Cambridge Elements

Elements in Historical Theory and Practice
edited by
Daniel Woolf
Queen's University, Ontario

MYTHS, HISTORY WARS, AND INDIGENOUS–SETTLER RELATIONS IN CANADA AND OTHER SETTLER STATES

David Bruce Amichand MacDonald
University of Guelph

Shaftesbury Road, Cambridge CB2 8EA, United Kingdom

One Liberty Plaza, 20th Floor, New York, NY 10006, USA

477 Williamstown Road, Port Melbourne, VIC 3207, Australia

314–321, 3rd Floor, Plot 3, Splendor Forum, Jasola District Centre, New Delhi – 110025, India

103 Penang Road, #05–06/07, Visioncrest Commercial, Singapore 238467

Cambridge University Press is part of Cambridge University Press & Assessment, a department of the University of Cambridge.

We share the University's mission to contribute to society through the pursuit of education, learning and research at the highest international levels of excellence.

www.cambridge.org
Information on this title: www.cambridge.org/9781009714211

DOI: 10.1017/9781009223188

© David Bruce Amichand MacDonald 2025

This publication is in copyright. Subject to statutory exception and to the provisions of relevant collective licensing agreements, no reproduction of any part may take place without the written permission of Cambridge University Press & Assessment.

When citing this work, please include a reference to the DOI 10.1017/9781009223188

First published 2025

A catalogue record for this publication is available from the British Library

ISBN 978-1-009-71421-1 Hardback
ISBN 978-1-009-22320-1 Paperback
ISSN 2634-8616 (online)
ISSN 2634-8608 (print)

Cambridge University Press & Assessment has no responsibility for the persistence or accuracy of URLs for external or third-party internet websites referred to in this publication and does not guarantee that any content on such websites is, or will remain, accurate or appropriate.

For EU product safety concerns, contact us at Calle de José Abascal, 56, 1°, 28003 Madrid, Spain, or email eugpsr@cambridge.org

Myths, History Wars, and Indigenous–Settler Relations in Canada and Other Settler States

Elements in Historical Theory and Practice

DOI: 10.1017/9781009223188
First published online: December 2025

David Bruce Amichand MacDonald
University of Guelph

Author for correspondence: David Bruce Amichand MacDonald, david.macdonald@uoguelph.ca

Abstract: Many Western settler states are undergoing processes to improve Indigenous-settler relations. The primary focus is Canada, with some discussion of Australia, Aotearoa New Zealand, and the United States of America. This Element highlights myths promoted by explorers, settlers, and the state about Indigenous Peoples and history. It engages with and attempts to correct a selection of the misperceptions that have developed over several centuries. I argue that the first "foundational history wars" were advanced by European explorers, travellers, and settlers through the promotion of negative myths about Indigenous Peoples, as an accompaniment to settler colonialism. I distinguish these from "modern history wars" from the 1960s to the present. The goal is to provide a fuller history that critically engages settler myths, privileges Indigenous perspectives, and offers a robust and informed critique of dominant historical narratives. The larger goal is to promote truth as a necessary accompaniment to reconciliation.

This Element also has a video abstract:
www.cambridge.org/EHTP_MacDonald_abstract

Keywords: Canada, history, Indigenous Peoples, settler colonialism, colonization

© David Bruce Amichand MacDonald 2025

ISBNs: 9781009714211 (HB), 9781009223201 (PB), 9781009223188 (OC)
ISSNs: 2634-8616 (online), 2634-8608 (print)

Contents

Introduction	1
Foundational and Modern History Wars: Conflict over Memory and Representation	7
Myths Against Indigenous Peoples	11
Myth of an Empty Beckoning Land	17
The Myth of Recent Asian Origins	18
Myths of a European Right of Discovery	20
Myth of Indigenous Peoples as Doomed Races	23
Myth of Treaties as Surrender Documents	28
Old-Fashioned Myths: Conflict, Cruelty, and Superstition	32
Myths Against Indigenous Women as a Justification for Colonization	35
Myths of Indigenous Alcoholism	38
Myths of Meritocracy and the Liberal Democratic (Racial) State	43
Myths of Meritocracy and Multiculturalism: The Colour-Blind Society	49

Québec and Indigenous Peoples: Distinctive Relations and Myths   53

Québec as a Victim Nation   57

Myth of an Indigenous "Métis" Nation   59

Conclusions: The Lengthy History of History Wars   60

Bibliography   62

Myths, History Wars, and Indigenous–Settler Relations 1

Introduction

Many Western settler states are undertaking processes to improve Indigenous-settler relations after centuries of colonization. The primary focus of this Element is Canada, with some discussion of other CANZUS countries, namely: Australia, Aotearoa New Zealand (ANZ), and the United States of America (USA). The term "reconciliation" has been widely used in Canada and Australia. It is optimistically interpreted by some as an opportunity to ensure that Indigenous lands are returned, and that political support and funding are available to promote the revitalization of Indigenous languages, cultures, spirituality, and self-determination. It can also be a time to heal and to make amends for negative legacies of the past, and to change settler colonial structures that demonstrably discriminate against Indigenous Peoples.[1] Others have a more critical view, seeing reconciliation as mainly performative, a chance for settler governments to rebrand themselves as inclusive and progressive, to make settler colonialism appear more palatable to everyone.[2] Still others deny there is any need for changes to the status quo. Indeed, offence is taken when it is suggested that the country is anything other than a model of equal opportunity, liberal democracy, and prosperity.[3]

Consonant with debates on reconciliation[4] (a focus of my previous work, although not a major topic of this study) are ongoing "history wars" about the nature of Indigenous-settler history and ongoing relations within and between communities.[5] This analysis foregrounds the conflicts between settler-based, often celebratory national narratives (which often accompany negative myths against Indigenous Peoples) and Indigenous Peoples and their supporters, who are more focused on challenging these narratives in the quest for historical accuracy and the realization of Indigenous rights. In a Canadian context, dominant historical accounts have at least one social purpose, primarily: to promote belonging for settlers of European origin. They cement close ties to the British and French mother countries of many settlers and demarcate the cultural boundaries into which (often racialized) newcomers are expected to integrate. Such narratives marginalize Indigenous Peoples so that national history is not based on any violent "original sin," but rather is a record of peaceful, consensual settlement. We see similar discussions in the US, Australia, and ANZ.

An underlying argument here is that European explorers, travellers, and settlers initiated the first "history wars" through the promotion of negative

---

[1] See for example TRC Canada, *Final Report*.   [2] See MacDonald, "Canada's TRC," 117–120.
[3] Flanagan, *First Nations? Second Thoughts*; Gilley, *Case for Colonialism*.
[4] MacDonald, "Canada's TRC"; MacDonald, "Paved with Comfortable Intentions."
[5] MacIntyre and Clark, *The History Wars*; Considine and Considine, *Healing Our History*.

myths about Indigenous Peoples, as an accompaniment to settler colonialism. These "foundational history wars" are understood here as the nineteenth century denial and denigration of Indigenous oral histories, laws, and practices of self-determination. The first iterations of such "wars" were very one-sided, marked by assertions of European and Christian superiority and benevolence. As Gina Starblanket (Cree/Saulteaux, Star Blanket Cree Nation) describes, the settler state has long advanced a dominant narrative that "colonial settlement was negotiated and governed legally and fairly," using non-violent means designed to "respect and cultivate ideals of human freedom and equality." However, such "Imperial approaches," Starblanket recalls, "have always been contested by Indigenous people, who have long pointed to more expansive understandings of the relationships we entered with the Crown and have undertaken sustained critique of violations of this relationship."[6]

Positive myths of settlement were often accompanied by the silencing of Indigenous voices. Silencing includes what Māori educator Liana MacDonald describes as "a racial discourse aligned with state ideologies ... that supports ignorance and denial of the structuring force of colonisation."[7] This process has also been called "colonial unknowing," an "aggressively made and reproduced" mode of disavowing the settler colonial past and its implications in the present.[8]

A series of contemporary or "modern history wars" took place predominantly from the 1960s. Indigenous perspectives have been more critical of mainstream histories than dominant settler accounts, in that they highlight centuries of land dispossession, the use of famine to force Indigenous Peoples onto reserves, the prohibition of languages, spiritual practices, and cultures, the suppression of traditional forms of diplomacy and trade, and the attempted destruction of Indigenous leadership and government.[9] However, these accounts often do not focus on victimization, but rather on the continued vibrancy and agency of Indigenous Peoples as political actors within, outside, and beside the settler state, with millennia of history in the exercise of self-determining rights and practices.[10] The emphasis has been on what the late Moana Jackson (Ngāti Kahungunu and Ngāti Porou) called an "ethic of restoration," on regaining the relationships and balance that have been threatened by ongoing processes of colonization. Crucial to restoring balance is the prioritization of Indigenous stories, rituals, practices, which also implies correcting the misleading stories

---

[6] Starblanket, "Red Ticket Women," Kindle 46 of 146.
[7] MacDonald, *Silencing and Institutional Racism*, 3.
[8] Vimalassery et al., "Colonial Unknowing," 1042.
[9] See for example Deloria, *Custer Died*; Cardinal, *Unjust Society*; Coulthard, *Red Skin*, Simpson, *As We Have Always Done*; Turner, *Not a Peace Pipe*; Stark, "Criminal Empire."
[10] Lightfoot, *Global Indigenous Politics*.

Myths, History Wars, and Indigenous–Settler Relations 3

Europeans have told for many centuries, stories integral to the dispossession of Indigenous Peoples.[11]

This Element identifies and de-normalizes mythistorically grounded racist beliefs, promoted by explorers, settlers, and the state about Indigenous Peoples and history. It attempts to correct a selection of the misperceptions that have developed over the centuries since the exploration, colonization, and settlement of the CANZUS states. The goal is to provide a fuller history that privileges Indigenous perspectives and offers a robust and informed critique of dominant historical narratives.

In many settler states including Canada, myths of peaceful settlement and consensual state formation have been challenged, as Indigenous Peoples gain prominence in national life, and articulate the case for self-determination, the return of lands, and control over their own affairs. These processes, ongoing for decades, are now resulting in tangible changes to national narratives, including recognition of settler state genocide against Indigenous Peoples (Canada, and the US state of California), and federal government support (albeit primarily rhetorical) for Indigenous self-determination. While Canada figures as the primary case study, this analysis also briefly discusses foundational myths in the other CANZUS countries: Australia, ANZ, and USA.

Methodologically, this study draws from documents primarily about Canada, distilled from primary sources written from the middle of the nineteenth century to the present, with some secondary sources as well. The author has identified recurring stereotypes, claims, and partial truths mixed with much misleading information, which together form a series of myths. These are then critically analyzed and refuted, using a combination of historical and contemporary accounts. Identifying and refuting settler myths is a process consistent with the work of contemporary Indigenous academics and community leaders. For example, Bob Joseph (Gwawa'enuxw) recently identified and refuted nine myths about Indigenous Peoples in Canada[12] while Roxanne Dunbar-Ortiz and Dina Gilio-Whitaker do the same for 21 myths about Native Americans in the United States. The myths they identify feed into what they call a "master narrative" about American history and its foundation, justifying systemic racism and ongoing colonization and structural violence against Indigenous Peoples.[13]

---

[11] Jackson, "Decolonization." See also Simpson, *As We Have Always Done*.
[12] Joseph, *Dispelling Myths*.
[13] Dunbar-Ortiz and Gilio-Whitaker, *All the Real Indians*. My work considers *some* similar myths, although I use different historical source material. See their myths: "Indians Were the First Immigrants to the Western Hemisphere"; "Columbus Discovered America"; "Indians Were Savage and Warlike"; "Indians Are Naturally Predisposed to Alcoholism," and "What's the Problem with Thinking of Indian Women as Princesses or Squaws?"

These myths are foundational, creating interlocking narratives that validate Western settlement at the expense of Indigenous Peoples. This Element proceeds with the following sections. First, it engages with "history wars" over the benign/malign foundations of the country, currently being undertaken in Canada and other western settler states, before turning to a discussion of how we can best understand the context of myths and racism directed against Indigenous Peoples.

The first set of myths described and refuted are attempts to demonstrate that Indigenous Peoples did not and do not possess legitimate claims to the lands and waters on which their ancestors have lived since time immemorial. First, there is the myth that the landmass of Canada is a relatively empty, beckoning land, with a small population. Second, since the ways in which lands were used by Indigenous Peoples did not conform to European forms of land ownership, there is therefore no legitimate Indigenous claim to territory. Similar myths were to be found in Australia, ANZ, and the US. Other cognate myths include the recent origins of Indigenous Peoples from Asia, alongside the peaceful and legitimate nature of European settlement and colonization. Treaties are presented as land surrender documents, as legal transactions where Indigenous leaders consented to the spread of settler government and the relinquishment of their lands and waters in return for a limited range of benefits from the crown.

A second set of myths (sometimes called old-fashioned prejudice) was specifically designed to denigrate Indigenous Peoples. The myth of the doomed race is one example, myths of Indigenous conflict, violence, and lack of civilization, another; both can also be found in other settler states. Equally widespread were myths about the mistreatment of Indigenous women by Indigenous men, amid a general denigration of traditional gender relations. These were often accompanied by myths of Indigenous alcoholism and the need for colonization and missionary conversion to protect Indigenous Peoples from their own excesses, as well as from the "bad" white men, who were contrasted to a range of "good" missionaries, police, and government officials.

A third set of myths relies on more modern forms of prejudice, often epitomized by claims that Indigenous Peoples demand more than their individual fair share of resources and recognition from the country. These myths stem from the claim that Canada is a successful liberal democratic society, a well-functioning meritocracy where everyone can theoretically attain positions of comfort and influence through hard work. The history and legacies of conquest, invasion, and genocide are suppressed in favour of myths of peaceful and collaborative settlement. Settler states can promote narratives of being democratic, tolerant, open, affluent, and multicultural, while at the same time maintaining systems which actively and paternalistically suppress Indigenous

Peoples. This section concludes by unpacking myths of meritocracy within a supposedly multicultural state, where difference is to be tolerated within a European settler framework.

The final section analyses a series of myths related to the province of Québec and their distinctive construction of a linguistic, cultural, and lineage-based nation. This nationalism excludes Indigenous Peoples and denies settler identity and responsibility for colonization. Many in Québec reason that they as French Canadians share similar experiences with Indigenous Peoples of being oppressed. This final section of myths includes compact theory, Québec as a French nation, Québec as the victim of English Canada, the myth of a kind Québec towards Indigenous Peoples, and finally, that genetically, French Canadians constitute a Métis nation.

Providing Some Background Context

Indigenous Peoples form a growing proportion of Canada's 40-million-person population. As per the 1982 Constitution, three classifications of "Aboriginal" peoples are officially recognized by the state: First Nations, Inuit, and Métis.[14] Indigenous Peoples are and have always been diverse, with over 70 languages, more than 630 First Nations, numerous groups as part of the Métis nation, and Inuit peoples divided into four regions and 50 communities.[15] The largest demographic group are First Nations with treaty status, with many having membership and access to one or more of the 3,394 reserves within Canada. Having status means in most cases being subject to the *Indian Act*, which has (with some exceptions) divided First Nations into bands, with elected band councils, a settler colonial-imposed administrative and political structure.[16]

Before proceeding further, it is useful to provide a short overview of European colonization in the Americas and other settler states, introducing some context for the rest of the study. The colonization of the Americas over five centuries involved multiple European powers (Including Spain, Portugal, Holland, England/Great Britain, and France), deploying a range of means to spread their political, economic, and legal power to the so-called new world. Processes of Christian conversion, forced assimilation, land theft, and many other activities led to the (at least partial) replacement of Indigenous forms of government and land stewardship with European forms. Indigenous Peoples lost most of their lands. In Australia, colonization took place later, primarily in the nineteenth century, but this island continent was the locus of considerable violence, including frontier massacres, bounties, warfare, and the spread of

---

[14] Galloway and Bascaramurty, "Census 2016."
[15] Statistics Canada, "Indigenous population."   [16] Palmater, *Beyond Blood*, 166–167.

disease. Aotearoa New Zealand was colonized in the nineteenth century, and also saw war and bloodshed, particularly during British-instigated wars of territorial conquest from the 1860s.[17]

Annie Coombs notes appositely that while the term settler may seem benign, it "masks the violence of colonial encounters that produced and perpetrated consistently discriminatory and genocidal regimes against the indigenous peoples of these regions."[18] Patrick Wolfe has referred to a "logic of elimination" as a key aspect of settler colonialism, where Indigenous societies are dissolved, to be replaced by "a new colonial society on the expropriated land base."[19]

Accompanying overt violence, various legal instruments were also deployed to divest Indigenous Peoples of their lands. With the exception of Australia, CANZUS states have used treaties to facilitate colonization. Aotearoa New Zealand has only the 1840 Te Tiriti o Waitangi, which covers the entire country, while Canada has over 70 treaties officially recognized between 1701 and 1923, with a further 25 "modern treaties" signed after this time. The United States negotiated and signed 368 treaties from 1777 to 1868. In all cases, treaties were not land surrender agreements, nor did they imply consent to dissolve centuries of Indigenous self-government and title to lands and waters. There are stark differences between Indigenous language versions and oral understandings of treaty (to which Indigenous Peoples acceded), and the English versions written down and disingenuously recognized under settler law.[20]

Positionality

This study is written by a biracial Indo-Trinidadian and Scottish settler. The author's ancestors on his mother's side came from Uttar Pradesh and Bihar from 1856 and were taken to and laboured as girmitiyas (indentured labourers) on three sugar estates in the rural south of Trinidad. They were mainly Muslim and Hindu, and many acquiesced to conversion by Christian missionaries to obtain a formal education. While Canada has been founded on whiteness and remains a settler state dominated by people of European origin, there is considerable demographic change. In the background of this study is the observation that racialized peoples can and do express solidarities with Indigenous Peoples and can experience racism. However, George Lipsitz's observation is accurate: white supremacy can be embraced and perpetuated by non-white peoples. There is a trade-off whereby outsiders can become insiders through the

---

[17] MacDonald, *Identity Politics*. [18] Coombes, "Introduction," 1–2.
[19] Wolfe, "Settler Colonialism," 388.
[20] MacDonald, "Indigenous Peoples and Self-Determination," 105.

exclusion of the most marginalised groups in society.[21] As Canada grows in population size, and more people like the author and his Trinidadian relatives settle here, we are not obliged to maintain Eurocentric narratives of the state, especially if they continue to act to the detriment of Indigenous Peoples. Similar decisions pertain for other CANZUS states, all of whom have growing Indigenous and non-European populations.

Foundational and Modern History Wars: Conflict over Memory and Representation

This section highlights what can conventionally be seen as the "history wars," which developed during the 1980s and 90s. These can be termed "modern history wars," whereas earlier "foundational history wars" took place as the country was being created and settled.

As conventionally understood, for at least four decades, CANZUS states have been the locus of competing narratives over whether the creation of their state was a benign, universally beneficial undertaking, or an inherently negative and genocidal exercise at the expense of Indigenous Peoples, and their traditional relations with lands, waters, and animals.[22] History wars can be defined as debates over collective memory within a national territory, between those separated by generational, ethnic, ideological or other divisions deemed to be of fundamental importance to members of the groups involved. "Modern history wars" are often prompted by catalytic events. They can develop when Indigenous Peoples, marginalized communities, and revisionist historians and activists seek to counter hegemonic approaches. Exposing the state's strategic forgetting of history is another crucial element.[23]

The term "history war" was coined in 1994, when the Smithsonian Institution planned to host an exhibition featuring a moral discussion about whether the US Air Force was justified in the atomic bombing of Japan in 1945. This inaugurated a rhetorical conflict, pitting so-called liberals against conservatives over whether political correctness had become too pervasive in American culture.[24] Modern history wars became more intense during historical flashpoints – especially commemorations of key signposts in settler history. These include: the 500th anniversary of Christopher Columbus' voyages in 1992, the Australian bicentennial commemoration of Captain Arthur Phillip's first fleet in 1988, the 150th anniversary of Canadian confederation in 2017, and the 250th anniversary of James Cook's landing in Aotearoa New Zealand. These celebratory

---

[21] Lipsitz, *Possessive Investment in Whiteness,* viii.
[22] MacIntyre and Clark, *The History Wars.*   [23] MacDonald "Canada's History War," 411–431.
[24] MacIntyre and Clark, *The History Wars*, 9, 220.

narratives were challenged by Indigenous Peoples with their own memories of these events and their genocidal legacies.[25]

In Australia, the genesis of modern history wars can be traced to bicentennial commemorations, for which Aboriginal and Torres Strait Islander protesters proposed "a year of mourning."[26] These took an important role in public consciousness from 1996 when Prime Minister John Howard condemned the use of "black armband history" to make the balance sheet of Australian history appear overwhelmingly negative when in his perspective the reverse was true.[27] Many Aboriginal and Torres Strait Islander Peoples and activists called out the Howard government for donning a "white blindfold" in its understanding of history.[28] A key focus of discussion was whether genocide was committed in the colonization of Australia, and indeed whether the entire history of the country was marked by continual but different and interlinked forms of genocidal violence. This included eighteenth and nineteenth century massacres and other colonial tactics, as well as the forcible removal of Indigenous children from their parents and communities in the twentieth century.[29]

In Canada, history wars developed in the 1980s and 1990s, largely as a debate between settler scholars about how to approach settler history. Michael Bliss and Jack Granatstein emerged as key figures in the debate between "inclusivists" and "nationalists" over the most desirable direction for Canadian history.[30] Of interest to this study was the later debate about the legacies of colonization in general and the Indian Residential Schools (IRS) in particular during the early 1990s and after. The IRS system was established in the mid-1880s, designed to assimilate Indigenous Peoples into a settler-dominated colonial society. The federal government worked closely with mainline Canadian churches, who were together responsible for running most schools until the 1950s. From 1920 until the 1950s, schooling for First Nations children aged five to sixteen was compulsory and the government saw to it that there were few if any day schools available near First Nations reserves. Children were forcibly removed from their families and communities, and efforts were made to destroy Indigenous languages, cultures, and identities.[31]

---

[25] Brantlinger, "Black Armband," 656; MacDonald, *Identity Politics*; Te Punga Somerville, *Two Hundred and Fifty Ways*.
[26] Brantlinger, "Black Armband," 656;
[27] MacIntyre and Clark, *The History Wars*, 3; Woolf, *Concise History of History*, 274.
[28] MacIntyre and Clark, *The History Wars*, 131; Brantlinger, "Black Armband," 657.
[29] Bartrop, "The Holocaust"; Moses, *Genocide and Settler Society*, 18.
[30] Christopher Dummit was the first to specifically use "history wars" in this context. See Chapnick, "Where Have?"
[31] MacDonald, *The Sleeping Giant Awakens*.

In 1990, prominent Anishinaabe leader Phil Fontaine (later National Chief of the Assembly of First Nations) openly declared how he was physically and sexually abused and encouraged others to come forward. Eventually, in 1991, the Royal Commission on Aboriginal Peoples was created to uncover and document the various harms committed against Indigenous Peoples. The Commission's *Report* in 1996 highlighted four main types, the first of which concerned widespread abuse in Residential Schools (as well as their goals of assimilation and cultural destruction).[32]

In 2009, the Truth and Reconciliation Commission of Canada began investigations into the full extent of abuses in the IRS system. In 2015 they concluded that cultural genocide was committed, and outlined 94 recommendations to bring about fundamental change to the settler status quo. Other federal government-funded initiatives followed, making important inroads into highlighting the structural racism of the state and its violent and sometimes lethal consequences. These initiatives include the National Inquiry into Missing and Murdered Indigenous Women and Girls (2016–2019), and the Office of the Independent Special Interlocutor for Missing Children and Unmarked Graves and Burial Sites associated with Indian Residential Schools (2022–2024).[33] Following a visit by the late Catholic Pope Francis in 2022, when the Pope acknowledged that genocide was committed in the IRS system, the Canadian House of Commons in October 2022 unanimously passed a non-binding motion recognizing the crimes of the IRS system as genocide. This admission is rare amongst settler states, and the only other CANZUS government to recognize genocide has been the US state of California, when in 2019 Governor Gavin Newsom used the term in his official apology to Indigenous Peoples. In neither case have governments initiated any new policies to reflect these admission of responsibility.

In understanding any conflict over memory and representation, it is crucial to ask who has the legitimacy to speak for the past. Daniel Woolf highlights how conflict can develop when the past is seen as the "property" of some but not others, and when there are underlying assumptions that some people have the moral or ethical right to "own" the past and interpret it as they think fit, advancing their own view as the only authentic voice.[34] Settler state myths have been dominant for at least a century and a half, if not longer, and European settlers have not been accustomed to having their understandings of history challenged by Indigenous Peoples or others, although within settler societies there are often vibrant (if circumscribed) debates.

---

[32] Cairns, "Coming to Terms," 77–78.
[33] Independent Special Interlocutor, *Sites of Truth*, 7–8.
[34] Woolf, *Concise History of History*, 275.

Challenging settler myths may serve as a useful corrective, reducing settler dominance over how knowledge is created and spread. Lisa Monchalin (Algonquin, Métis, Huron) describes how: "General Canadian history has typically minimized or rationalized the realities of colonization," and when settlers learn about some elements of colonization, there is a tendency for them to distance themselves from the wrongs of the past.[35] Settlers promoting a conservative view of the nation and its founding may denounce purportedly new narratives as disloyal and distorted portrayals of the past. Often there is a sense that personal and collective identities are threatened when national narratives seem to be under sustained critique for being partial, misleading, or false.[36]

While the majority of Canadians: Indigenous, settler, and arrivant (descendants of Black and other people brought to the Americas against their will),[37] appear to support some progressive change, there is also backlash. In 2018, the Canadian polling firm Angus Reid charted a division over Indigenous issues between, with those very much against any distinct rights for Indigenous Peoples at 21 percent (the "Hardliners") with the "Wary" and "Sympathetic" comprising exactly 50 percent of the population, followed by "Advocates" at 29 percent.[38] While there may be little *modus vivendi* between Advocates and Hardliners, it is instructive that half of Canadians fall in the middle. History wars involve persuasion – presenting the past and present in such a way that readers, listeners, participants, can be encouraged to take a position and mobilize politically, either to bring change or reinforce the status quo.

Those denying negative aspects of Canadian history may express nostalgia for a European past, through the belief that accounts from previous centuries (written before "wokeism" and political correctness "tainted" freedom of speech) are a more authentic depiction of Indigenous Peoples and Europeans.[39] The general argument advanced in this study is that Canada was constructed by earlier more hardline versions of today's Hardliners who engaged in foundational history wars to promote the merits of European colonization and settlement. Negative myths built the country as it is currently constituted. In modified form, the same political parties and institutions have run the country over the past century, and Canadian institutions have not changed in any fundamental way, despite much hopeful rhetoric about overcoming the past and forging new and better relationships.[40] Unfortunately, our

---

[35] Monchalin, *The Colonial Problem*, XXI.
[36] MacDonald "Canada's History War," 411–431; Carleton et al., "Misuse of Indigenous and Canadian History."
[37] Byrd, *Transit of Empire*. [38] Angus Reid, "Truths of reconciliation."
[39] Duchesne, *Canada in Decay*. [40] Manuel and Derrickson, *Reconciliation Manifesto*.

country was built on foundations of the denial of Indigenous humanity and civilization, and contemporary denialism continues a long tradition. This is also true in other CANZUS states.[41]

Myths Against Indigenous Peoples

This Element advances that anti-Indigenous myths provided a permission structure for European settlers to move into someone else's traditional territories and feel secure and justified in doing so. Myths, as Henry Tudor recalled some time ago, can serve social functions, "either to advocate a certain course of action or to justify acceptance of an existing state of affairs."[42] Myths are bound up with practical arguments, such as supporting "the claim of a certain group to hegemony, sovereign independence or an extension of territory."[43]

For Alex Zakaras in his study of foundational myths, clear contrasts are made between the positive characteristics of the group (its virtues, idealized attributes, and values) and "others" who are seen to be threatening, antagonistic, or potentially: a "source of pollution or decay against which struggle was and is necessary."[44] Zakaras traces settler state consolidation to the development of coherent national myths, able to bind settlers together, "creating new forms of collective identity, of fusing often diverse and far-flung groups with competing cultural, ethnic, and religious attachments into a cohesive national people."[45] People thus become invested in their myths because these assume fundamental significance to the nation during periods of uncertainty. Chiara Bottici adds that a political myth doesn't just reproduce what is understood about a given group: "it can also be the means for the construction of an identity yet to come."[46]

Myths helped create order, routine, and some level of predictability and understanding of the human condition. Most myths contain elements of truth, as Joseph notes, but due to the fact that they are often developed for one group and against another, they are also misleading, and can "paint a distorted picture that does not represent reality."[47] Jackson too notes the central role of myths in colonization, "stories that range from pseudo-scientific and legal rationalisations to blatantly racist presumptions."[48] In many respects, myths have played a useful psychological role for settlers, streamlining decision-making for those in the dominant group. Less thought is required, and context can pragmatically be ignored. Indeed, one can employ myths to reassure oneself that what on the

---

[41] MacDonald, *Identity Politics*. For a detailed analysis see Carleton et al., "Misuse of Indigenous and Canadian History."
[42] Tudor, *Political Myth*, 124.   [43] Tudor, *Political Myth*, 139.
[44] Zakaras, *American Individualism*, 12.   [45] Zakaras, *American Individualism*, 13.
[46] Bottici, "Rethinking Political Myth," 3.   [47] Joseph, *Dispelling Myths*, 3.
[48] Jackson, "Decolonization."

surface seems extremely unequal and intolerant treatment is in fact normal, unremarkable, and the natural order of things, what Mark Rifkin has identified as "settler common sense."[49]

Eviatar Zerubavel notes the prevalence of denial in most societies, stemming from the individual's "need to avoid pain," especially so when "something particularly distressful threatens our psychological well-being."[50] Indeed, people may engage in "a conspiracy of silence," where they choose to outwardly ignore a reality known to them all, but which is never discussed in public.[51] This can lead to what Steven Newcomb (Shawnee/Lenape) terms a process of "reification," in which "a colonising nation or people will tend not to interpret or characterise its political system as one of domination." Indeed, he observes: "The descendants of those who managed to impose their political system forcibly on nations and peoples now termed 'Indigenous' ... undoubtedly prefer to frame that system in terms of 'democracy' and 'civilisation'."[52] These processes enable the flourishing of positive narratives of the state, like Paulette Regan's critical dissection of Canada as a "nation of peacemakers," which supports a "myth of innocence" over how and why an Indigenous presence has until recently, been virtually erased from mainstream history and society.[53]

Promoting positive narratives of the settler state, deploying negative myths against those who would undermine it, while simultaneously supressing difficult knowledge, are all part of the how settler states have operated against the sovereignty and wellbeing of Indigenous Peoples. Aileen Moreton-Robinson (Goenpul Quandamooka) has described the "great deal of work [necessary] to maintain Canada, the United States, Hawai'i, New Zealand, and Australia as white possessions." Indeed, she identifies conflicts for spatial recognition taking place in every urban landscape of the settler state where "signs of white possession are embedded everywhere." By contrast, she reminds us that "Indigenous sovereignties exist here too," even if settler states try to obscure this evidence.[54]

Those supporting mainstream foundational myths may not have malign intentions, and historically, settlers have found it difficult to gain the information and perspective necessary to critically engage with the status quo myths they are being fed. A goal of identifying and refuting anti-Indigenous myths is thus to better educate the settler public, to inform and persuade, so that no one can continue to plausibly deny the negative aspects of colonization and their

---

[49] Rifkin, *Settler Common Sense*.   [50] Zerubavel, *Elephant in the Room*, 5–6.
[51] Zerubavel, *Elephant in the Room*, 2.   [52] Newcomb, "Domination in Relation," 21.
[53] Regan, *Unsettling the Settler within*, 106.
[54] Moreton-Robinson, *The White Possessive*, xi, xiii.

continued legacies. Joseph puts it that sharing "knowledge and information" has mutual benefit, and "can make the world a better place for Indigenous and non-Indigenous people."[55] A change in mentality can have obvious benefits for Indigenous Peoples. Allan and Smylie note the pervasive nature of racism in government policy documents, educational systems, and through media stories, "contributing to and reinforcing a naturalized kind of racism that permeates Canadian society." Negative views in turn, "all serve to justify acts of belittlement, exclusion, maltreatment or violence at the interpersonal, societal and systemic levels."[56]

Classifying Race and Racism

Systematized conceptualizations of race accompanied European colonization. One of the first was a study by François Bernier in 1684, followed by Carolus Linnaeus' 1735 classification of four distinct racial groups, with the "Americanus" peoples identified as "aggressive." Johann Blumenbach in 1779 would divide humanity into five races, including American Indians. Much of this work elevated the white European "Caucasian" as superior to other racial groups. The theory held that humanity could be divided into biological races, each possessing distinct and unchangeable inherited characteristics. Further, there was a hierarchy of superior to inferior races reflected in the rules of social, legal, and political systems. Inequitable treatment of different racial groups was justified on the basis of each race's differing potential. Social divisions, distancing, and specific rights could be allocated or withheld based on perceptions of difference.[57]

Studies focused on Indigenous Peoples as targets of settler racism often differentiate between "old-fashioned prejudice," and "modern prejudice."[58] Old-fashioned prejudice might be understood as based on perceived "characterological defects," and can be manifest in openly hostile ways, while more modern types of prejudice can be subtle and insidious, focusing instead on the belief that Indigenous Peoples exaggerate problems to make illegitimate demands on the state. Tied to modern prejudice is the belief that settler society has nothing to feel sorry about or responsible for, since people today cannot be held culpable for the injustices of the past.[59] An initial review of range of old-fashioned prejudices is followed with an analysis of more modern types. Both feed into and support negative myths about Indigenous Peoples, which can be

---

[55] Joseph, *Dispelling Myths*, 2. [56] Allan and Smylie, "First Peoples," 3.
[57] Reading, "Understanding Racism."
[58] Morrison et al., "Old-Fashioned and Modern Prejudice," 293; 300.
[59] Morrison et al., "Legacy of Derogation," 1002.

seen as mythhistorical frameworks into which specific more narrowly defined prejudices can be fit.

Considerable effort has been undertaken for decades to classify and compare different varieties of racist myths against Indigenous Peoples, most of which are interlinked.[60] A key focus has been on structural racism and how it is manifest through negative outcomes in healthcare, the judicial system, in education, employment, housing, and other contexts. Through dissecting different types of settler attitudes, the belief is expressed that to understand and systematize may be crucial in ending anti-Indigenous racism. A 2008 study identified 108 negative descriptors of how Indigenous Peoples were regarded in settler society, divided into three categories, the largest being personality traits, followed by a much smaller number of behavioral and physical characteristics.[61]

Indigenous Peoples are often written out of mainstream historical accounts, including Canadian school textbooks and curricula.[62] As a number of studies conclude, the targeting of Indigenous Peoples can take place through commission (myth-making, stereotyping, prejudice, and barriers) or through omission, where Indigenous Peoples are excluded and made to seem invisible or irrelevant to contemporary settler society.[63]

This Element focuses on mythhistorically grounded racist myths that have accompanied European colonization and settlement in Canada, and other settler states such as the USA, Australia, and ANZ. The focus is older myths, many drawn from a critical reading of primary sources: textbooks, memoirs, reports, historical, and government documents from the mid to late-nineteenth century to the present. These relate to similar myths in the more contemporary period, demonstrating how many of these negative views remain embedded in Canadian political consciousness.

Of importance to this study is that myths were and are to be found across the Canadian political spectrum. Socialists and self-professed anti-Fascists on the left, Liberals in the middle, and Conservatives to the right of a shifting centre have all promoted similar forms. Polling suggests that Canadian Conservative Party supporters are less likely to embrace some forms of Indigenous rights, and similar views pertain amongst National Party and ACT supporters in ANZ, and the Liberal/National Coalition and One Nation in Australia.[64] This was not always the case. Left and centrist paternalism towards Indigenous Peoples could

---

[60] For a recent discussion see Davis-Delano et al., "Representations of Native Americans"; Fitzgerald, *Native Americans on Network TV*; Lopez et al., "The Same, Yet Different"; Anderson and Robertson, *Seeing Red*.
[61] Morrison et al., "Old-Fashioned and Modern Prejudice," 282; 285–287.
[62] For a comparative discussion, see Schaefli et al., "Securing Indigenous Dispossession."
[63] See an overview in Davis-Delano et al., "Absence Makes the Heart Grow Colder".
[64] O'Sullivan, "Treaties, Truth and Equality."

sometimes be equally as harmful. Pragmatically, any governing party has a vested interest in appealing to settler voters, and in promoting settler-focused economic, political, social, and legal systems. Even parties who have been broadly sympathetic to Indigenous self-determination and overtly welcoming of a reconciliation agenda have also displayed major policy contradictions, and have failed to deliver much of what they promised.[65]

Many of the myths reviewed here operate from the tacit assumption that settler colonies and settler states were constructed according to universally beneficial meritocratic principles. Deniz Canel-Çınarbaş and Sophie Yohani define the myth of meritocracy as "the perception in the dominant culture that those who work hard and who have merit can succeed in life and in the society."[66] By contrast, those who fare poorly in society must have something inherently wrong with them, individually and/or collectively. Claims of Indigenous inferiority were often used to legitimate the creation of European-style settler states and to explain the often-obvious gaps between settlers and Indigenous Peoples when it came to who benefited from these newly imposed systems. Assumptions of meritocracy are woven throughout many settler myths, which note Indigenous decline but claim it to be inevitable, unless Indigenous Peoples fully embrace European ways.

Many of the myths outlined in this Element portray Indigenous Peoples as victims and passive recipients of settler benevolence or mistreatment. A goal of this analysis is to critically problematize these claims. Many Indigenous scholars caution settlers to avoid the trap of depravity narratives, what Eve Tuck (Unangax̂, St. Paul Island) terms "damage-centered research" and "deficit models."[67] Tuck calls for research which centres the strength and "survivance" of Indigenous Peoples within a context of colonialism, occupation, and genocide.[68] Indeed, over the many centuries of colonization, Indigenous Peoples fought back when it was expedient to do so, and retreated when it was not. They negotiated when they could, and the used their intelligence-gathering to warn of impending danger.[69] Their population numbers grew, defying the expectations of colonial administrators and commentators.

At the same time, it is important not to assume that the settler state was as powerful historically over the lives of its peoples as it is today. We can understand many settler myths as performative: they advanced a misleading narrative of settler strength and stability, when often the reverse was true historically. As Coombs stresses, settler identities were often fragile, with

---

[65] Manuel and Derrickson, *Reconciliation Manifesto*.
[66] Canel-Çınarbaş and Yohani, "Experiences of Microaggressions," 54.
[67] Tuck, "Suspending Damage," 12; 409.   [68] Tuck, "Suspending Damage," 415; 422.
[69] Ostler, *Surviving Genocide,* 8.

settlers caught between their refusal to integrate into the Indigenous realities in which they found themselves, choosing instead to maintain their European cultures and myths of origin, while simultaneously creating local settler institutions that were often viewed contemptuously by the colonial metropolitan centre.[70]

Elsbeth Heaman reminds her readers that Indigenous Peoples controlled much of the territory of what became Canada well into the nineteenth century and were recognized as powerful political actors with the ability to exert their self-determining interests.[71] Further, Heaman notes the fragility of the Canadian experiment: "the land was reluctant and the people were resistant. Indigenous people remained crucial power-brokers everywhere."[72] The threat of Americanization was a constant, and the nascent Canadian country was "a weak power in the shadow of stronger powers," and "continually in danger of state failure and/or conquest."[73] As such, the myths discussed here are in part aspirational, and an exercise in "boosterism" – the effort by would-be colonizers to encourage more Europeans to settle on Indigenous lands through the downplaying of hardships and the embellishment of opportunity.

Perhaps the first example of this genre was *History of Canada* (1855) a highly influential school history textbook by John McMullen, that went through several editions. The author desired to create a history of Canadians as a coherent community with common struggles and interests. Indigenous Peoples were presented as no impediment to colonization, since they were in his view, lacking in civilization, technology, political, economic, and social organization.[74] After a lengthy discussion of virtues and vices attributed to Indigenous Peoples, McMullen assured his readers that the "war-whoops" had now been replaced with the "church bell" and the "matin song of the milkmaid and the blithesome whistle of the ploughman." In short: "A poor and thinly scattered community of improvident savages, has been succeeded by an orderly, industrious, and enterprising people, whose genius and resources embody all the germs of a mighty nation." The future lay with the settler and Canada's destiny to become a powerful nation on meritocratic and white racist principles. The replacement of Indigenous Peoples by settlers should be no cause for lamentation, and Canada must have "little room for regret that the possession of her soil, has been transferred to the Anglo Saxon race, and that the rule of the fierce Indian has forever passed away."[75] McMullen's aspirational thinking as far as settlement was concerned, with his near-total denigration of Indigenous

---

[70] Coombes, "Introduction," 4. [71] Heaman, *Civilization*, 17–18.
[72] Heaman, *Civilization*, 21. [73] Heaman, *Civilization*, 27.
[74] For a useful analysis and background see Taylor, *Promoters*, 153–154.
[75] McMullen, *History of Canada*, xiv.

Peoples, helped establish a template for future books, while also distilling and reproducing various myths that had already been present.[76]

Myth of an Empty Beckoning Land

A key myth of North America during the nineteenth century was the demographic emptiness of the continent. Much of this study's research focus is on the Plains, what would become the Prairie Provinces (formerly Rupert's Land at the time of the formation of Canada in 1867). Such myths were used to justify the expansion of settler control over Indigenous territories, while Indigenous land holdings were reduced to a small fraction of their former size. The myth of a numerically small number of Indigenous Peoples helped justify state expansion, given that European migration numbers were large: 1.14 people million migrated to Canada from 1987 to 1914.[77] Reducing the numerical size and territorial reach of Indigenous Peoples were important considerations in justifying this rapid transfer of Europeans to Canada. Equally important was the view that Europeans could claim the right of discovery as the first civilized Christian peoples to explore and inhabit the landmass which would later be called Canada, through what is often called the doctrine of discovery.[78]

A key myth held that the future Prairie provinces were sparsely populated by peoples with no governance capability and little understanding of civilization. This section presents these writings in loose chronological order, from the early to mid-twentieth century. British-born writer and historian Emily Weaver's *A Canadian History for Boys and Girls* (1919) promoted myths of a "black-haired, copper-coloured people ... thinly scattered all over America." Weaver's history recounts Indigenous Peoples as backward, using "clumsy stone hatchets and shell knives," to engage in "picture-writing – that is, they made rough sketches instead of writing words."[79] While Indigenous Peoples were an interesting historical curiosity, Weaver assured her young readers that they were "few in number, and, in Canada, are found chiefly on lands set apart for them by the government and in the unsettled regions of the north and west."[80]

Further to this was the claim that Indigenous Peoples had no concept of politically bounded territory, and certainly no institutions of statehood in a European Westphalian sense that could compete with the sovereignty claims of the British. H.G. Mellick, Superintendent of Baptist Missions (1909) penned this description: "The [Indigenous] race was like sailors who were shipwrecked and drifted in many directions."[81] Percy Evans in his 1914 history of the Prairie

---

[76] Taylor, *Promoters*.   [77] Savoie, *Canada*, 132.
[78] Miller et al., *Discovering Indigenous Lands*, 4.   [79] Weaver, *A Canadian History*, 6–7.
[80] Weaver, *A Canadian History*, 7–8.   [81] Mellick, *Indians and Our Indian Missions*, 1.

Provinces noted the "scattered and migratory tribes of Indians who were allied in loose confederacies," claiming "The boundaries of their hunting grounds were thus constantly changing." They were, he avers, "confined to no precise territory." Settlers could therefore feel no compunction in taking over these lands for farming, since it was unlikely they "were ever very numerous," and at any rate lived "a purely nomadic existence."[82]

Humourist and political scientist Stephen Leacock's later views epitomized a sense of Canada as an empty land, reflecting his blend of conservatism and imperialism. In his 1941 book, he observed that North America "remained, as it had been for uncounted centuries, empty." While conceding that "prehistoric North America [w]as inhabited by the Indians," he was quick to note that "Indians were too few to count," and their "use of the resources of the continent was scarcely more than that by crows and wolves, their development of it nothing."[83] The overarching description of Indigenous Peoples as nomadic reduced the impact of their territorial or sovereignty claims. Equally, in his 1943 historical account of the Prairies, Joseph Scott noted: "of course the boundaries of the land claimed by the tribes were not like the boundaries of countries, for the Indians had to move from place to place hunting the animals which supplied them with food."[84]

A primary focus of these myths was to deny sovereignty to Indigenous Peoples. The belief that Indigenous Peoples did not own land nor exercise political functions and create institutions in ways analogous to their European counterparts was proof that they had no government, and therefore no right to exercise self-determination.

The Myth of Recent Asian Origins

From the nineteenth century and into the present, a prominent myth about Indigenous Peoples was their recent Asian origin, journeying to what became Canada through no particular intention, and with no plans to establish permanent foundations of settlement or governance. These claims came at a time when Chinese and Japanese immigration was severely restricted. Journalist and historian Howard Kennedy (1925) painted the "Indian" as "a wanderer," slowly moving from Asia, fishing and hunting with no plans to settle. Rather, they "don't know where they are going, and don't much care. They are not looking for a place to settle down in, land of their own to farm, to build a house on." Thus, they had no ambitions akin to European settlers and were never to be considered competition for the abundant resources available to the growing

---

[82] Evans, "History of the Prairie Provinces," 32. [83] Leacock, *Canada*, 19.
[84] Scott, *Our Prairie Provinces*, 39.

country. Kennedy recalled: "These first comers have 'discovered America,' without knowing it. They have no idea that they are the first to set foot in a 'new world.' ... They just go on living as they have been used to living."[85]

Newer but nevertheless cognate perceptions of Indigenous Peoples have been promoted in current the Canadian citizenship guide, *Discover Canada*, crucial reading for all those writing the citizenship exam. First published under the Conservative government of Stephen Harper in 2012, it has remained substantially unchanged in its 2021 incarnation (the most recent edition). Rather than engage with settler colonialism, prospective citizens are told that Indigenous Peoples are the first immigrants, given that their ancestors "are believed to have migrated from Asia many thousands of years ago." Discussion of Indigenous governments and territorial claims are reduced to their being "well established here long before explorers from Europe first came to North America."[86]

In terms of Indigenous history, no sense of territorial ownership, attachment, or government is recognized. Rather: "When Europeans explored Canada they found all regions occupied by native peoples they called Indians." Their ownership of distinct territories was not discussed. Instead, they are described as "liv[ing] off the land, some by hunting and gathering, others by raising crops." Discussions of colonial violence are set aside for a vague description of the commonplace nature of warfare amongst "Aboriginal groups as they competed for land, resources and prestige." Europeans brought change which on balance turned out well, stresses the guide. On the negative side "Large numbers of Aboriginals died of European diseases to which they lacked immunity." No other causes of death are mentioned, and the story ends happily, as "Aboriginals and Europeans formed strong economic, religious and military bonds in the first 200 years of coexistence which laid the foundations of Canada."[87]

Whether readers encounter older myths or their more contemporary manifestations, both make the case for settler ownership and sovereignty over lands on which Indigenous Peoples had lived for millennia. The focus here was what became known as the "doctrine of a legal vacuum." Brian Slattery critiques what he terms the myth of Indigenous "wanderers" who "possess[ed] neither sovereignty nor permanent rights of any sort to the territories they occupied." Indigenous Peoples would present a practical obstacle to colonization, but in legal terms, posed no more of a challenge than "the wild animals of the forests and plains."[88]

---

[85] Kennedy, *Book of the West*.   [86] Canada, *Discover Canada*.   [87] Canada, *Discover Canada*.
[88] Slattery, *Ancestral Lands*, 3. See also Borrows, "Ground-Rules."

Myths of a European Right of Discovery

Selected European myths from the fifteenth century onwards promoted European Catholic forms of control at the expense of Indigenous ownership of their own territories in the so-called "New World." The original Catholic "doctrine of discovery" harkens back to the fifteenth century, designed to legitimate a global Papal jurisdiction, and any actions necessary to increase Papal influence, including the Crusades and the invasion and conquest of non-Christian lands.[89] A series of Papal "Bulls" (declarations) such as the Inter Caetera (1493) legitimated the conquest of territory and its control by a Catholic monarch, if local populations were "infidels" and "barbarian nations" who had yet to be converted. The Treaty of Torsedillas (1494) territorially divided the "New World" between Spain and Portugal under the guise of converting Indigenous populations. Conversion also became a legitimating factor for the French and the English as they expanded into what later became North America. In 1541, the French king's commission to explorer Jean de la Rocque included spreading the "Holy Catholic Faith and Catholic Doctrine" as part of the colonizing process. By 1578, English letters patent to explorer Humphrey Gilbert provided authority for him to "discover ... such remote, barbarous, and heathen lands, countries, and territories not possessed by any Christian prince or people nor inhabited by Christian people and the same to have, holde, occupy and enjoy."[90]

The English (and later British) would distinguish their forms of conquest as superior, by claiming to deplore the violence of the Spanish and Portuguese. Overt religious motives would be sidelined in favour of arguments stressing European style land occupation and cultivation as the deciding factor in whether Indigenous Peoples owned their own land and possessed sovereignty. Paul DePasquale traces English justifications for colonization to Thomas More's *Utopia* (1516), wherein the author outlined how lands could be taken "[w]hen any people holdeth a piece of ground void and vacant to no good or profitable use."[91]

As Barbara Arneil has explained, this theoretical proposition would be enhanced by John Locke, in his particular view of colonization in *Two Treatises of Government* (circa 1689). He rejected Spanish forms of violent territorial conquest and offered instead a series of tests based on rationality and how peoples lived on and related to land. Locke would successfully advocate for a "superior" English Protestant style of proprietorship based on agriculture, industrialization, and trade. Arneil traces a crucial change in the seventeenth

---

[89] Miller et al., *Discovering Indigenous Lands*, 4.
[90] Crawford, *Argument and Change*, 140–141.   [91] DePasquale, *Natives and Settlers*, xxiv.

century, when the focus of English colonialism shifted from colonial resource exploitation and trade to English settlement and occupation of Indigenous territory in the Americas. The perception of Indigenous Peoples thus changed from being indispensable trading partners to constituting impediments to colonial development.[92]

Reflecting this new attitude to colonization, Locke sought to create a new definition of property. Rights by virtue of occupation were now to be superseded by proof of ownership through particular types of labour: "[T]hose who tilled, enclosed, and cultivated the soul would be its owners."[93] By contrast, "natural" or "savage" people did not have any rights to property, and in Locke's conceptualization, Indigenous Peoples were both "superstitious" and "idle."[94] His myths were self-serving, and Locke had conflicts of interest, as he profited from the expansion of English agriculture, and the trade in enslaved Africans.[95] In order to operationalize the theory, Locke ignored much in his representation of Indigenous Peoples. Examples of their sophisticated settlements, successful cultivation and farming practices, as well as their entirely reasoned rejection of private property in favour of communal ownership were all suppressed in favour of a mythology that Indigenous Peoples were "nomadic but social, who lacked industry and reason, but had potential for both and knew little about cultivating the land or governing [themselves]."[96]

Tied to a Lockean sense of property was the right of discovery. A "settlement thesis" was established, through which British colonizers presented Indigenous nations as being uncivilized and therefore not worthy of consideration as sovereign entities. The concept of *Terra Nullius* held that there was a jurisdictional vacuum that could be filled by the Crown when they "discovered" and then occupied Indigenous lands. This has been dubbed the discovery paradigm, through which Indigenous rights including "Aboriginal title" flow only from Crown law, and thus are seen to be legally inferior to the sovereign powers of the Crown.[97]

A typical example of this thinking can be found in George Bryce's 1887 *Short History of the Canadian People*. Bryce was a Presbyterian minister, president of the Royal Society of Canada, and founder of Manitoba College.[98] Europeans claimed Canada by right of discovery, he noted, starting with "a Frenchman of Brittany," then "English adventurers on Hudson Bay," followed by the "restless

---

[92] Arneil, *Locke and America*, 2; 9; 15; 203.   [93] Arneil, *Locke and America*, 18–19.
[94] Arneil, *Locke and America*, 202.   [95] Arneil, *Locke and America*, 16–17.
[96] Arneil, *Locke and America*, 202.
[97] Hoehn, *Reconciling Sovereignties*, 1–2; Borrows, *Recovering Canada*, 117–118.
[98] He was also the brother of Dr Peter Bryce, whose famous report in 1922, *The Story of a National Crime*, did much to expose the federal government's inaction to the sickness and deaths of Indigenous children in Indian Residential Schools.

Scottish pioneers," and "American loyalists." The story of Canada, which largely excluded Indigenous Peoples was of a "gathering of the races" from several European countries, and their consolidation into one people, operating "under the shelter of Britain," to eventually assume control of "well-nigh half of North America."[99]

Similarly, Mercer and Robertson's *Public School History of England and Canada* (1886) avoided Indigenous Peoples almost entirely, and their section on the "discovery" of America focused on Columbus, while paying homage to the "hardy Norsemen," and later to Jacques Cartier.[100] Similarly, in *The Imperial Heritage* (1898), Ernest Williams stated that Canada "is ours by right of discovery," largely through the voyages of John and Sebastian Cabot, which were commissioned by the English King Henry VII.[101] The argument here central to this myth was the lack of European-style private land ownership, which denied Indigenous Peoples recognition of their control of lands and waters, as well as their governing capacity.

Throughout the history of English and British settlement in what is now Canada, the doctrines of discovery and *Terra Nullius* proved central to legitimating the theft of Indigenous lands and the eventual creation of the settler state.[102] Despite numerous court decisions challenging these doctrines, they continue to underwrite crown assumptions of state sovereignty and denial of underlying Aboriginal title. As John Borrows (Chippawas of the Nawash) has noted: "It requires a discriminatory denigration of Indigenous peoples' laws and ways of life to hold that Indigenous title and governance is subject to non-Indigenous paramount interests as a by-product of European sovereign assertions." In the end, we are left with an unresolved legal problem: "Crown power can be directly traced to discriminatory assumptions rooted in European sovereign assertions when the Crown 'discovered' Canada."[103]

In 2023, Pope Francis repudiated the doctrine of discovery, although he did not rescind the Papal bulls on which it was based, nor did he assume Vatican responsibility for their outcomes. Indeed, he claimed that the doctrine was not "part of the teaching of the Catholic Church," and was "manipulated for political purposes by competing colonial powers."[104] Soon after, the Canadian government released a statement noting how the doctrine constituted "a failure of the Catholic Church to uphold the inherent human rights of Indigenous Peoples," while affirming that the federal government "accepts that ancient doctrines such as this have no place in Canadian law and do not define our

---

[99] Bryce, *Short History*. [100] Mercer and Robertson, *History Primer*.
[101] Wiliams, "Imperial Heritage," 130131. [102] Miller et al., *Discovering Indigenous Lands*, 9.
[103] Borrows, "Durability of Terra Nullius," 725; 741. [104] Holy See, "Joint Statement."

Myths, History Wars, and Indigenous–Settler Relations

ongoing relationships with Indigenous Peoples."[105] Despite these admissions, however, little has changed in terms of the unbalanced power dynamic between the Canadian settler state which continues to assert crown title, and Indigenous Peoples who have considerably less control over their traditional territories.

Myth of Indigenous Peoples as Doomed Races

The myth that Indigenous Peoples were doomed to disappear was common in the nineteenth century and lent to settler colonialism a sense of historical inevitability. In North America, historians noted the frequent use of "vanishing" as a trope. The romantic ideal of "melting away" suggested that the "disappearance" of Indigenous Peoples, while unfortunate, was really no one's fault. One might abstractly blame historical inevitability and a Darwinian belief in evolution and "progress."[106] Late nineteenth-century settler anthropologists drew clear distinctions between what they saw as "primitive" versus "modern" societies. Indigenous Peoples were presented as resistant to change and consigned to antiquity, with anthropologists seeking to document their traditional beliefs and practices, within a context of inevitable decline and disappearance. By contrast, European political and cultural evolution and ascendency would be documented from an entirely different perspective. As Bain Attwood and Fiona Magowan have recounted: "In this grand narrative of progress, 'primitive,' oral societies such as Aboriginal ones tended to be precluded since it was held that they were neither capable of change nor compatible with modernity and therefore irrelevant to a study that traced the past becoming the present."[107]

That Indigenous Peoples supposedly lived poorly and would inevitably die out was taken for granted by some early (and extremely racist) commentators. Hugh Gray's *Letters from Canada* (1809), for example, described Indigenous Peoples as "*half* naked, *wholly* covered with dirt, and oily paints, and swarming with vermin; diminutive, and weakly in their persons and appearance." Grey took their passing for granted: "their numbers decrease every year, if they were wholly extinct, I do not think that human nature would be a great sufferer by it."[108]

In Canada, a low tolerance for Western disease and "virgin soil epidemics" was used to excuse the very high death rates of Indigenous Peoples on reserves and in Indian hospitals and residential schools. Sherene Razack observes that as settler colonization proceeded, Indigenous Peoples were marked "materially and symbolically," as bodies who were "not up to the challenge of modern life,"

---

[105] Canada, "Statement Doctrine of Discovery."
[106] Wilson, *The Earth Shall Weep*, xxii–xxiii; 45; Dippie, *The Vanishing American*.
[107] Attwood and Magowan, "Introduction," xvi. [108] Gray, *Letters from Canada*, 158–159.

reinforcing settler claim's to be the "legitimate heir to the land."[109] The subtext here was that Indigenous Peoples were part of a pre-colonial past, a pre-civilized environment, and thus did not belong in modern settler colonial society.

Julian Ralph, in a 1892 collection of historical sketches, lamented the passing of Indigenous Peoples as regrettable but inevitable. His book began with a type of false praise for the supposedly carefree Indian, which he contrasted to the European. Civilization, he remarked, brought with it "many rules and responsibilities and so much hard work." This he contrasted to the life of the "wild Indian," who possessed "the greatest amount of pleasure and the least share of the care that men can hope for." Western civilization doomed Indigenous Peoples, and while sad, was not really anyone's fault. Ralph reminisced: "They lived in their war-paint and by the chase. Now they are caged. They live unnaturally and die as unnaturally, precisely like other wild animals shut up in our parks."[110]

Methodist missionary John Maclean (1896) provided a more global historiographical appraisal of "doomed" Indigenous races. In his comparative history, there was "a tendency to extinction among all savage nations, and notably amongst the American tribes who are the heirs of a deteriorating civilization."[111] This was not unique however, given "evidences of decay" "amongst the tribes on every island and continent," including Indigenous Tasmanians, Australians, Hawaiians, Māori, and Fijians.[112] Much of this appraisal, as Ralph later revealed, was an argument for missionary conversion as well as Indigenous assimilation into farming and industrial life throughout the British Empire.

Similar mythology could be found elsewhere. In Australia, overtly racist views held that Aborigines were fated to disappear due to their putative inferiority, according to eighteenth century accounts, as "one degree above brute creation," "the lowest race in the scale of humanity," "the connecting link between man and monkey tribe," and "a species of ... tail-less monkeys."[113] In ANZ, Māori were often cast as a model or superior Indigenous People. For novelist Anthony Trollope, they were "the most civilised" of all "savages," and in racial hierarchies, Māori were usually placed just under Europeans, above Aborigines and southern Africans. Imagery of Māori as "selected stock" who had braved long voyages to reach New Zealand prompted such epithets as "Vikings of the Sunrise" and "Aryan Māori."[114] This however did not prevent some European theorists concluding that Māori too were destined to disappear,

---

[109] Razack, *Dying from Improvement*, 193.   [110] Ralph, *On Canada's Frontier*, 16.
[111] Maclean, *Canadian Savage Folk*, 286.   [112] Maclean, *Canadian Savage Folk*, 286–288.
[113] Cited in Laidlaw, "European Settlement," 69.   [114] Sinclair, *A Destiny Apart*, 197–199.

and belief of the inevitable "passing of the Māori" was exemplified through missionary John Wohlers' 1881 prophesy that "As a race they had outlived their time."[115] Belief in Māori disappearance could be found at least as far back as 1835, when the "British Resident," James Busby noted that Māori themselves felt their demise was inevitable: "[T]hey conclude that the God of the English is removing the aboriginal inhabitants to make room for them."[116]

Given myths about the decline of Indigenous Peoples, then, it was important for settlers to model gratitude and paternalistic kindness because they would inevitably inherit and control whatever good things Indigenous Peoples had discovered or invented. This performance of gratitude signalled the passing of ownership from the original inhabitants to the new and more worthy inheritors of the land. Kidd outlined in *Canadians of Long Ago* that while their "old life is now almost gone," it is crucial that settlers remember the "gifts which the Indians have given us." This included showing trails and canoe routes, providing food and shelter, and pemmican, all of which "helped greatly to make exploration easier."[117]

Within the Canadian Department of Indian Affairs, the myth of doomed Indigenous Peoples remained salient for some time, although by the of the nineteenth century, it was a theme waning in importance. Superintendent General Clifford Sifton wrote in his 1904 *Annual Report*: "It seems difficult in some quarters to get rid of the idea, at one time doubtless quite justified, that the Indian is a dying race, doomed to extinction before the advance of civilization, but facts and statistics fail to support this view of the situation." He nevertheless noted that despite advances and his own optimism, "In so far as some few tribes are concerned it would appear as if there were something endemic in their constitution ... which suggests their ultimate disappearance, unless it can be discovered and remedied."[118]

The tone of this myth was somewhat regretful, but also optimistic in terms of the prospects for European newcomers. Indigenous Peoples were fated to disappear, and therefore, there was no need for settlers to plan long-term institutions that could incorporate them as equals. Nor would it be necessary to create syncretic institutions to somehow combine Indigenous and European elements that could bridge different governance and legal traditions. Instead, the myth implied European cultural and (often assumed) racial superiority. As such, while one might personally lament the situation, little could be done to go against the inevitable forward march of history.

---

[115] Pool, *Te Iwi Māori*, 58–60. For further discussion see Barta, "A Very British Genocide."
[116] Barta, *A Very British Genocide*, 61. [117] Kidd, *Canadians of Long Ago,* 172.
[118] Indian Affairs, "Annual Report 1904."

Newer Iterations of the Doomed Race Myth

A number of "hardline" Canadian settler authors continue to promote negative myths from the past. The "stone age" thesis remains popular amongst some who have sought to denigrate Indigenous societies to make their assimilation into Euro-Canadian life both inevitable and desirable. A widely cited example of this type of thinking is Frances Widdowson and Albert Howard's presentation of Indigenous Peoples as constant financial dependents on the state. Having merely reached the "paleolithic or Neolithic stage" versus Europeans with "thousands of years of civilization," inevitably the weaker gives way to the stronger. The authors engage in a string of what could be termed racial slurs to explain the problems of Indigenous communities, including, *inter alia*, their "undisciplined work habits, tribal forms of political identification, animistic beliefs, and difficulties in developing abstract reasoning." Assimilation seems for them the best way forward.[119]

Similarly, for the publisher Conrad Black, Indigenous cultures were "stone age," and Indigenous Peoples could, with some exceptions, be described as "nomads, clothed in hides and skins, living in tents, surviving on fish and game, and usually at war, which included the torture to gruesome death of prisoners from other tribes and nations, including women and children." Black ended his analysis of Indigenous history with the conclusion: "even the First Nations should be grateful that the Europeans came here."[120] Along similar lines, Bruce Gilley, in his unambiguously titled *The Case for Colonialism*, also cites "the Stone Age level of development," as a primary causal factor in Indigenous decline, alongside "the disease and warfare that scattered their numbers."[121] Similar arguments have been advanced by right of centre commentators in Australia and ANZ for several decades.[122]

The best-known example of this genre is Tom Flanagan's *First Nations? Second Thoughts* (2019). Flanagan, a former advisor to Canadian Conservative Prime Minister Stephen Harper, portrays Indigenous decline as predictable, given that Europeans were "several thousand years more advanced ... both in technology and in social organization." This civilizational gap meant that "the European colonization of North America was inevitable and, if we accept the philosophical analysis of John Locke and Emer de Vattel, justifiable." Presumably, he agrees with these sentiments. That Indigenous Peoples possess the right to sovereignty and self-determination is denied by Flanagan, due to their inferior level of political organization. Tribal *communities*, he argued, can

---

[119] Widdowson and Howard, *Disrobing the Aboriginal Industry*, 11–13, 25–26.
[120] Black, "Canada's Treatment."   [121] Gilley, *Case for Colonialism*.
[122] See for example Minogue, "Aborigines," 13–15; Plover, *New Zealand*.

never have the sovereign power of European style *states or nations*. To accept the myth that First Nations are real nations with the right to self-determination, Flanagan worries, would be to turn Canada into "a modern version of the Ottoman Empire."[123] These views denigrate Indigenous Peoples and their capacity to govern themselves, while similarly denying that they ever possessed this capacity.

Contemporary Indigenous scholarship fundamentally challenges myths of recent arrival, introducing new conversations that problematize the inherently political goals of presenting Indigenous Peoples as recent arrivals from Asia who seemingly aimlessly occupied the Americas. Cree-Métis archeologist Paulette Steeves has traced Indigenous presence in what is now North America to somewhere around 130,000 years ago, and potentially over 200,000 years ago. The territory from which they originated was not "Asia" at that time, and there were no Asian cultures per se when these migrations in the ancient past took place. Steeves focuses on evidence proving the longevity of Indigenous Peoples in the Americas, in the face of concerted Western archaeological efforts to erase that status, to "cleave our links to the land." Her work outlines European settler political agendas behind the mythologizing of Indigenous Peoples as recent arrivals, and she critiques earlier archeological efforts as being the political product of settler amateurs with little scientific training. Archeology as a discipline has been tied to settler colonial goals, and she calls for recognition that "deeper time frames and links to the land legitimize Indigenous peoples' ownership of the land and makes them more human."[124]

Overall, myths of a sparsely populated continent, by relatively new arrivals, with few indicators of long-term well-developed civilizations, helped justify colonization and the taking of lands. Claims of recent arrival from Asia or elsewhere, Steeves notes, create "scenarios where contemporary Indigenous peoples' links to ancestors and lands are suspicious or nonexistent."[125] By contrast, if we accept the presence of Indigenous Peoples in what is now the Western Hemisphere for tens of thousands of years, we "put them on equal footing with areas of the so-called Old World." A goal then is to trace an origin point for the development of Indigenous identities, a much earlier time: "This land is where their cultures and lifeway were born; this is where they are from."[126] Steeves' work is by no means accepted by the settler mainstream, but it is an innovative and persuasive example of how history is being actively debated and discussed, and how European settler researchers are having their credentials and objectivity critically examined. The argument is a very

---

[123] Flanagan, *First Nations? Second Thoughts*, 6–7.   [124] CBC, "Indigenous Archaeologist."
[125] Steeves, *Indigenous Paleolithic*, xix.   [126] Steeves, *Indigenous Paleolithic*, 187.

important one: the longer Indigenous Peoples have been in the hemisphere, the more legitimacy they can claim as distinct peoples with their own origin stories rooted on their ancestral lands, and their own self-determining histories.

Myth of Treaties as Surrender Documents

Tied to myths of a sparsely populated continent, was the myth that the treaties eventually signed in some parts of Canada between some Indigenous nations and the crown constituted land and sovereignty surrender documents. The predominant myth promoted by the federal government has been of treaties as, one-time transactional rather than ongoing relational agreements.[127] Implicit too was the assumption that there were no valid treaties between Indigenous nations (from a Western perspective) before these land surrender agreements were initiated.

A 1967 publication by the Indian Affairs clearly articulated the surrender myth. The treaty-making process was contextualized as a response to Indigenous unease "at the influx of settlers," the reduction of the bison (buffalo) and general concerns for the future. Treaties from 1870 are undertaken with benevolence on the part of the crown, to provide security for Indigenous Peoples through "the extinction of Indian title." From this period onwards, First Nations leaders supposedly gave up land and sovereignty. Treaty 1 (August 1871) was described as a surrender document for a large tract of land in southern Manitoba. Treaty 2 was described as a "surrender from the Chippewa Indians" of several tracts of land. Treaty 3 was also described as the ceding of land; Treaty 4 was the "surrender of a tract of land." Later treaties used similar language, with the government generally outlining the terms of the treaties to include "the relinquishment of the Indian right and title" to specific lands. As a result: "The Indians had permission to hunt in the ceded territory and a fish in the waters thereof, as long as it remained the property of the Crown...."[128]

The treaties, according to this myth, involved the surrender of land and sovereignty to the British (later the Canadian) crown, in return for various benefits from the state, including permission to hunt on the ceded territories, to fish, gain some annuities, and live on some lands aside for reserves and farms. Other benefits included agricultural implements, farm animals, sometimes healthcare, and provision for the establishment of schools on reserve.[129] By 2023, the federal government continued the same argument, seeing the 11 numbered treaties as "land surrenders on a huge scale," bringing Indigenous Peoples in the view of the government "under the jurisdiction of the Dominion

---

[127] On this see Borrows, "Ground-Rules"; Johnson, *Two Families*.
[128] Canada, *Indians of the Prairie Provinces*, 8–10.
[129] Canada, *Indians of the Prairie Provinces*, 10.

of Canada and its laws." While noting that some Indigenous leaders were unhappy with the arrangements, there is certainly no attempt to refute the land surrender claims.[130]

The focus here was legitimating European forms of governance. The myth of surrender assumed that Indigenous Peoples recognized that they would inevitably disappear, and that their lifestyles and traditions were civilizationally inferior. The myth assumes that Indigenous leaders sought to sign treaty in order to guarantee the survival of their people within a European institutional structure. We know from Indigenous oral histories and the work of Indigenous treaty scholars that the myth is untrue. Treaties were to form the basis for ongoing and enduring relationships between treaty partners. They offered the potential for treaty federalism that could bring together Indigenous and settler orders as distinct governments but in ways that were mutually beneficial.[131]

That Indigenous nations were self-determining political actors was affirmed by the British Crown through the 1764 Treaty of Niagara, signed with numerous Indigenous nations. The Treaty recognized Indigenous ownership of the land and premised further British settlement on Indigenous consent. It established clear lines of authority, and it gave the British Crown responsibility for keeping local colonial administrations in line so they would not bother Indigenous Peoples in the practice of their governments and in their use of their resources and lands. At Niagara, Two Row Wampum belts were exchanged, conveying for Indigenous Peoples an "understanding of a mutual relationship of peace and non-interference in each other's way of life," as John Borrows described it. The treaty's oral implications recognized Indigenous self-government and sovereignty.[132] The Covenant Chain belt, also part of the treaty process, depicted two individuals holding hands, representing distinct peoples who were also interdependent.

These periods of treaty-making coincided with the relative strength of Indigenous Peoples. Early agreements dealt with peace, friendship, and trade, and they were often conducted on terms of equality, carefully observing Indigenous diplomatic protocols, such as smoking a calumet, exchanging gifts, intermarrying to promote kinship relations, and other means. Later periods of treaty-making from the late eighteenth century were marked by a decline in Indigenous power and land holdings, and a commensurate increase in the relative power and size of European populations.[133]

---

[130] Canada, "Numbered Treaties."
[131] See Ladner, "Treaty Federalism"; Henderson, "Empowering Treaty Federalism."
[132] Jai, "Bargains Made," 121–122; Borrows, "Wampum at Niagara."
[133] Lo Wang, "Broken Promises."

From Canada's first Prime Minister John A. Macdonald onwards, settler governments engaged in patterns of obfuscation, and employed translators who equivocated the surrender clauses of treaties when negotiating terms with Indigenous leaders.[134] Contra the myth outlined in the previous section, Indigenous leaders never agreed to an absolute surrender of territory, which was neither part of the vocabulary nor the conceptual worldviews of Plains peoples.[135] For example, the Cree word for sale is "Atawagiwa," which is never used for land, while terms for land transfer are "eskonigan (to share) or kitieynamatin (to yield for use)."[136] This conforms loosely to the European legal concept of usufruct, whereby someone may enjoy the use and benefit of a property even if it is owned by someone else. Sharon Venne (Notokwew Muskwa Manitokan) clarifies that male Indigenous leaders who took treaty had neither the power nor the mandate to surrender territory. Leaders represented and followed the directions of their community, and did not have the legitimacy to sign away "the land, water, trees, mountains, resources above and below the ground, animals, birds, fish and all other living things."[137]

Gordon Christie (Inupiat/Inuvialuit) notes a fundamental contradiction between Indigenous views of sovereignty and that of the Crown. He writes: "Indigenous communities and nations continue to assert *independent* legal and political authority over their lands, waters, and peoples, while we see presumptions in Canadian law and policy that indigenous legal and political authority either no longer exists, or that to the extent it does there's no longer independent, that it is "merged" into crown sovereignty."[138] This was Crown mythology, and no such legal surrender of territory by Indigenous nations took place. Sheldon Krasowski's detailed analysis of the first seven numbered treaties on the Canadian Prairies demonstrates that the oral agreements and the notes of the negotiations are very clear. Chiefs on behalf of their people agreed to land sharing relationships in return for treaty benefits from the crown: "including annuity payments, reserved lands, education, and assistance with the transition to agriculture." However: "they certainly did not surrender the land. It was to remain Indigenous."[139]

In Canada, the desire of Indigenous First Nations, individually and through collective bodies, to have the Crown honour its treaty commitments has continued. A good example is the 1978 "Position Paper" by the Federation of Saskatchewan Indians (which represents Indigenous nations in this province):

---

[134] Krasowski, *No Surrender*, 2.
[135] Cardinal and Hildebrandt, *Treaty Elders*; Starblanket, "Numbered Treaties," 11.
[136] Gray, "Onion Lake," 37. [137] Venne, "Introduction," 6.
[138] Christie, "Reconciliation," 37. [139] Krasowski, *No Surrender*, 2.

In the treaties, we did not surrender our right to govern ourselves.... We are claiming our right, guaranteed by our treaties, to survive as a distinct political and cultural entity within Canada. ... At no time have we ever agreed to the proposition that the Canadian state had the right to regulate the internal affairs of Indian governments.[140]

By 2010, the (slightly renamed) Federation of Saskatchewan Indian Nations again articulated this perspective: "Indians retained the right to govern themselves. The Treaty process did not diminish Indian Government but rather confirmed its existence. When the Government negotiated with the Chiefs and signed the Treaty documents they were recognized as legitimate leaders of legitimate bodies."[141] The Assembly of First Nations (the national lobbying organization for Canadian First Nations) has maintained the same view, while engaging in what might be described as creating their own myths about Europeans. Their *Constitutional Report* (1992) described First Nations as "The founding people, because their ancestors were living here on turtle island, with their own laws and institutions, before the Celts swarmed over Britain and the Gauls invaded what is now France."[142]

Indigenous Peoples had millennia long-histories of making treaties before the Europeans arrived. They developed complex and sophisticated cultures and systems of governance, law, and defence, as well as trade networks and military alliances. They maintained diplomatic protocols that involved the exchange of gifts, ceremonies such as pipe smoking, the negotiation of treaties, and they kept records of these diplomatic activities in a wide range of forms.[143] Of the early treaties, the Indigenous-led Yellowhead Institute notes that they "reflected a world where diverse communities should share a geography if they collectively worked towards co-managing the contents of the bowl or dish, "as long as the grass grows" or "the world stands."[144] Many examples exist. Venne cites the pre-colonial Cree-Dene Treaty which demarcated specific territories for each nation on either side of the Peace River and continues to be honoured.[145] Aimée Craft (Anishinaabe-Métis) carefully outlines the historic alliance system between three Anishinaabe nations (The Council of Three Fires) as an example of an enduring treaty relationship. This Council in turn maintained long-term alliances with others nations like the Iroquois (Haudenosaunee) and the Sioux (Dakota).[146]

Further to these forms of human diplomacy, Indigenous Peoples also have a long history of treaty-making with non-human living beings. Human-to-human

---

[140] FSIN, "The Indian Act," 18–19. [141] FSIN, "Saskatchewan Treaty Land Entitlement," 7.
[142] AFN, *First Nations Circle*, 1. [143] Palmater, *Indigenous Nationhood*, 1.
[144] Yellowhead, "Treaty-Making." [145] Venne, "Treaties," 2.
[146] Craft, *Breathing Life*. Kindle 13 of 93.

treaties were but one iteration of a long-term complex process involving mutual relationship-building founded on principles of enduring respect and reciprocity. For Yellowhead, relationships with animals were central to the survival and identity of the nation:

> The treaty between the Anishinaabe and the deer and the moose sought to repair the harm from overhunting; the treaty with the beaver was about knowledge exchange around childcare. Each ascribed agency and self-determination to these animals, treaties between equals designed to promote sharing, respect, and mutual autonomy.[147]

Treaties with Europeans can through this optic be understood as bringing newcomers into a web of long-term treaty relationships. Canada's assumption of responsibility for interpreting treaty, has resulted, Gina Starblanket observes, in "incoherent," and "misinhabited" interpretations. These fail to recognize Indigenous understandings of treaty as "frameworks for relating," representing "diplomatic processes for negotiating relations of non- violent and generative co-existence between living beings in shared geographies."[148] These points articulate that the final goal of treaty-making was not European-Indigenous relationships but sense of balance and reciprocity between all inhabitants of a particular territory. This view can provide a deeper historical context for understanding the significance of treaty in many Indigenous nations.

Old-Fashioned Myths: Conflict, Cruelty, and Superstition

This section of the Element may be triggering for readers, because it outlines racist views, designed to strike a combination of fear, revulsion, and pity in settler readers.[149] Such myths presented Indigenous Peoples as irrational, cruel, and childlike. The upshot was that they could not govern themselves and thus needed Europeans to intervene with Western order and government. These myths stressed the desirability and necessity of European government and law, and suggested that Indigenous Peoples did not have the capacity to govern themselves in ways which were peaceable, predictable, and civilized. The focus therefore was creating a system based solely on European conceptions of good governance.

The myth of the warlike and cruel Indian was commonly found in European traveller accounts and school textbooks. British major George Warburton (1857) outlined: "The rudest form of human society known in the old world,

---

[147] Yellowhead, "Treaty-Making." [148] Starblanket, "Numbered Treaties," 2, 14.
[149] The following sections contain numerous racist myths and racist terminology directed towards Indigenous Peoples. The offensive language may trigger some readers. Please exercise your best judgment.

was far advanced beyond that of the mysterious children of the West, in arts, knowledge, and government."[150] John Bourinot's *Canada* (1897) featured a section on Indigenous Peoples, who were derided for their "savage nature," animated by "animal passion" and lacking in "the purity of love." He wrote: "Prisoners were treated with great ferocity, but the Iroquois exceeded all nations in the ingenuity of torture. Stoicism and endurance, even heroic, were characteristics of Indians generally ... "[151]

William Clement's *History of the Dominion of Canada* (1897) described Indigenous men as being "of unclean habits and without morals," noting: "Upon the war-path he was cruel, tomahawking, scalping and torturing with fiendish ingenuity. A stoic fortitude when himself tortured was about his only heroic quality."[152] Historian George Wrong's work (1935) continued a similar theme: "[S]ome tribes practised revolting cruelties and it was true of most Indians that they were lazy, dirty, vain and arrogant."[153] Indigenous Peoples, he argued, had no regard for British conventions of war. Indeed, in their warfare, "primitive conditions" created a code which "justified anything in order to kill the enemy ... They tortured to death and even ate prisoners." As such, he appeared to find little problem with the fact that "[a]ll this caused in the British officers the angry conviction that the only good Indian was a dead Indian."[154]

These views were also prevalent in Canadian government publications. For example, Superintendent General of Indian Affairs Frank Oliver, in his *Annual Report* for 1910, described an Indigenous "indifference to human life and suffering," which "still to no small extent pervades the Indian population." His hope was that "dissemination of Christianity and expansion of the somewhat curtailed limits of their knowledge and interests may gradually work a change in this regard."[155]

It is worthwhile considering the eminent positions of many of these commentators, who represented part of the intellectual elite of the settler state at that time. Bourinot served as chief clerk of the Canadian House of Commons, and helped found the Royal Society of Canada (the preeminent organization of academics), of which he was later its president. Clement was a retired judge based in British Columbia, while Wrong was an ordained Anglican minister, a fellow of the Royal Society and head of the Department of History at the University of Toronto. These men were some of the architects of Canadian

---

[150] Warburton, *Conquest of Canada*, 62.   [151] Bourinot, *Canada*, 124.
[152] Clement, *History of the Dominion*, 13
[153] Wrong, *Canada and the American Revolution*, 80.
[154] Wrong, *Canada and the American Revolution*, 75.
[155] Canada, "Annual Report 1910," xxii.

academic life and contributed to the cultural foundations for how the country was imagined and settlement justified.

Myths of Superstitious Child-Like Indigenous Peoples

The desire to spread European Christianity as an accompaniment to colonization prompted a wide range of anti-Indigenous myths, related to their spiritual beliefs and practices. Clement in his 1897 account conveyed a typical perspective: "Indian religion was purest superstition, people forest, stream and air with supernatural beings, both good and evil."[156] In *Red Indians I Have Known* (1919) Anglican missionary James McCullagh employed a range of insults to enjoin Indigenous Peoples to abandon their spiritual beliefs and practices:

> In that darkness there may be laughter, it is true, but it is the laughter of the idiot; there may be joy, but it borders on frenzy; there may be pleasure, but it is only animal; happiness there is none. From the cradle to the grave everything is make-believe, and the whole atmosphere of life is a lie.[157]

The demonization of Indigenous Peoples and their spiritual practices was widespread in mainstream literature, especially in the work of missionaries. Government documents reflected similar perspectives. James Allan Smart, Deputy Superintendent General (1899) observed that: "While a considerable number of Indians still refuse even nominal adherence to Christianity, their superstitions and cognate rites, such as the celebration of Potlaches or Sun Dances, have been denuded of their most objectionable features, and are fast falling into disuse, as are also the kindred practices of their medicine men."[158]

It was often claimed by Europeans that Indigenous Peoples were like children, unable to make rational decisions for themselves. Painter George Catlin's 1890 book promised his would-be youthful readers that Indigenous Peoples: "are *children* – like yourselves, in the many senses of the word. They are without the knowledge of arts of civilized man." This called for some degree of paternalism: "In their relationship with civilized people they are like orphans. Governments who deal with them assume a guardianship over them, always calling them their 'red children'; and they, from their childlike nature, call all government officials in their country 'Fathers.'"[159] The state was thus enjoined to act as a paternalistic ward to the Indians, leading them along the path of Western civilization.

The belief in childlike and irrational Indigenous Peoples was embedded in legislation. Certainly, there was no provision for Indigenous involvement in

---

[156] Clement, *History of the Dominion*, 13.
[157] Mcgullagh, *Red Indians*, 3.
[158] Canada, "Annual Report 1899," xxxi.
[159] Catlin, *Life among the Indians*, 19.

Confederation in 1867, and Indigenous leaders were not at the bargaining table. A subclause to section 91 of the British North America Act (1867) gave the federal government responsibility for "Indians and Lands reserved for the Indians."[160] The government began dissolving Indigenous governments and outlawing cultures and ceremonies, while taking land and stripping Indigenous nations and governments of their political, legal, and economic power. The federal government also arrogated the power for itself to define who was or was not an "Indian," and could strip Indigenous Peoples of their "status." John A. Macdonald was clear that Indigenous Peoples were to be considered akin to "persons underage, incapable of the management of their own affairs," and treated accordingly.[161] They therefore became in law, wards of the government, akin to minors "incapable of looking after their own interests and in need of the protection of the state." As such the government withheld citizenship, denying them the right to vote, stand for public office, purchase alcohol, and gain land under the settler-focused homestead system.[162]

Myths Against Indigenous Women as a Justification for Colonization

Throughout North America's long history of colonization, gender myths have been used against Indigenous Peoples, with Indigenous women as particular targets of violence.[163] Traditional Indigenous matrilineal societies were especially targeted by patriarchal colonizing government officials and missionaries. In Canada, the Indian Act legally alienated many Indigenous women from their communities, while creating and implementing an elected band council system dominated by men. The National Inquiry on Missing and Murdered Indigenous Women and Girls (2019) engaged in a detailed study of gender myths, to document why Indigenous women and girls were targeted with violence and death at a rate almost six times higher than their white counterparts. The Inquiry noted the evolution of three historically predominant myths which are still influential today. The "Queen" image depicted an older woman, "militant and mothering," a strong matriarchal figure. Second was the "Indian Princess," a more sexual, girlish, female figure, more easily subject to assimilation and cooption. Indigenous women came to symbolize "virgin land that was open for consumption to settlers."[164]

With the occupation and takeover of Indigenous lands, together with Indigenous resistance, the third image of the "squaw" was used to justify

---

[160] Savoie, *Canada*, 125.   [161] TRC Canada, *Final Report*, 106–108.
[162] Francis, *Imaginary Indian*, 202–203.
[163] For a detailed history and discussion see Deer, *The Beginning and End of Rape*.
[164] NIMMIWG, *Reclaiming Power and Place*, 386.

territorial colonization, through the belief that Indigenous Peoples were uncivilized. As the Inquiry notes: "The term "squaw" literally means dirty, immoral, and unworthy; it is the antithesis to the traditional Victorian woman." It was used to justify mistreatment and violence against Indigenous women, who were stereotyped as unfit mothers who could not care for their children. As well, the image of "easy squaws" helped promote unchecked violence, permitting "Indigenous women to be blamed for the sexual deviance of white settler men."[165] The National Inquiry documented the long history of hyper-sexualization of Indigenous women, especially the false belief that they were promiscuous. This served the interests of settler men who could feel justified in demonstrating racism, while also sexually assaulting them.[166]

At times, Indigenous women were seen as a hindrance to Indigenous men when the state sought to civilize or "advance" them. For example, a 1909 House of Commons *Sessional Paper* would target Indigenous women: "No sooner do the men earn some money than the women want to go and visit their relations on some other reserve, or else give a feast or dance to their friends .... The majority of (the women) are discontented, dirty, lazy and slovenly."[167] The perpetuation of negative myths about Indigenous women helped justify their mistreatment, and as the Inquiry notes, "relieved officials, police, and non-Indigenous settlers of all blame – or at least of any crime."[168]

At other times, Indigenous men were the focus of attack, with women portrayed as hard-working but long-suffering victims. Warburton's 1857 account is an early example of this racist genre. Indigenous men were accused of "loiter[ing] away their time in thoughtless indolence," refusing to do "the necessary industries" of life to the extent that "the greater part of the labor is performed by women, and men will only stoop to those portions of the work which he considers less ignominious."[169]

Bryce, in his *Short History* similarly identified amongst Indigenous Peoples "a strong sentiment as to the inferiority of woman," who functioned as "the slave of the family." He continued: "Woman must strike the tent and erect it, must do the great share of the burden-bearing on the march, must paddle the canoe on the voyage and portage the cargo about the rapids – she, in short, but attends the footsteps of her stalwart lord, like the spaniel, to fetch and carry."[170] Maclean's account (1892) was little different: "Amongst the Blackfeet, marriage is simply a bargain between the suitor and the young woman's father, for

---

[165] NIMMIWG, *Reclaiming Power and Place*, 386.
[166] NIMMIWG, *Reclaiming Power and Place*, 256.
[167] NIMMIWG, *Reclaiming Power and Place*, 255.
[168] NIMMIWG, *Reclaiming Power and Place*, 256. [169] Warburton, *Conquest of Canada*, 73.
[170] Bryce, *Short History*.

a certain number of horses." And: "When the husband became angry with his wife, he beat her with impunity; when he wished her no longer, he sold her, and when she was found guilty of adultery, her nose was cut off."[171]

In his 1901 *Story of the Dominion* John Hopkins claimed that Indigenous man, "treated his women as do all savage peoples, and considered himself far superior to the necessities of labour or servitude."[172] The myths, needless to say, where not rooted in fact. As David Smits noted many decades ago, such gendered misperceptions were often a form of European self-denial and a projection of their own sexism, with Indigenous Peoples as a "negative reference groups representing exact counter-images of Euroamericans' ideal sexual statuses and roles."[173] Smits put it down to a mixture of envy and resent, used to obscure the reality that settler women were not well treated and had fewer rights in their society than did Indigenous women in theirs.[174]

The National Inquiry highlighted serious problems of gender violence in Canada, including within Indigenous communities. Some Indigenous commentators make the argument that this must be first understood as the ongoing and intergenerational product of colonization. In a recent intervention, Mi'kmaq social worker Cyndy Baskin refutes the myth that there is some characterological defect that manifests itself in violence towards women. Rather, she traces an "ethic of domination" as the primary causal factor, attributing intimate violence to colonialism, assimilation, and cultural genocide.[175] Engaging with the histories and legacies of colonization helps put this violence into context: "economic and social deprivation, substance misuse, multigenerational and collective trauma, the breakdown of healthy family life, and the theft of traditional values."[176] Her understanding of traditional views holds that "family violence rarely existed prior to the breakdown of traditional societies caused by colonization." Women and men were seen as equal, albeit with different roles and responsibilities. Women were sacred because of their ability to give life, and the role of women as first teachers was in no way inferior to the role of men who were tasked with providing for and protecting the people.[177]

Intergenerational violence due to internalized patriarchal colonial norms and patterns means that solutions to violence against women may need to involve changes within Indigenous communities as they prepare for self-determination. Rauna Kuokkanen (Sami) articulates the case for ending colonization and patriarchy simultaneously, as both "relations of domination" are "nested," founded on "violence, unequal social and material relations, and deeply held,

---

[171] Mclean, *Indians of Canada*, 26. [172] Hopkins, *Story of the Dominion*, 44.
[173] Smits, "Squaw Drudge," 281. [174] Smits, "Squaw Drudge," 282.
[175] Baskin, "Systemic Oppression," 149. [176] Baskin, "Systemic Oppression," 153.
[177] Baskin, "Systemic Oppression," 154.

sometimes unconscious beliefs." Otherwise, expressions of Indigenous self-determination could perpetuate settler colonialism, even within Indigenous-led institutions.[178] Kuokkanen's focus is on stopping both forms of violence together, as solving one without addressing the other will be counterproductive. This is not to romanticize or essentialize Indigenous societies as entirely free of gender inequality, as some were more matriarchal and egalitarian than others. However, there is overwhelming evidence that most Indigenous societies had much stronger matriarchal traditions than anything Europe had to offer at that time.[179]

Myths of Indigenous Alcoholism

Like the previous characterological attacks, myths of an Indigenous predisposition for alcohol were instrumental in disparaging their rationality and responsibility, reducing their agency, in favour of arguments for settler state control of Indigenous bodies and communities. The idea that they were temperamentally unfit to govern was key, and these myths were also used to justify removing children from their families and communities. The myth held that Indigenous Peoples had a low tolerance for alcohol, coupled with an almost insatiable desire to consume it. These myths were widespread throughout the former British Empire and helped promote the merits of colonization.[180] In a Canadian context, myths of alcoholism were commonly promoted by white travellers, missionaries, and other commentators. Such views were widely found in school textbooks, government documents, and in the media. These were examples of sedimented prejudices which made the case for more settler colonialism, more surveillance and policing. Saving Indians from themselves became a strong justification for the expansion of missionary activity, the spread of state control, the reduction in lands for Indigenous Peoples and the denigration of their laws, governance, and spiritual practices.

These myths exaggerated the numbers of people susceptible to alcohol abuse, and conspicuously ignored environmental factors (loss of lands, community, employment, and freedom) that created the conditions for alcoholism to spread. Further, such ingrained views were never based on any comparative assessment of settler drinking habits. Alcohol consumption was weaponised against Indigenous Peoples by the state, through the passage of the 1857 Gradual Civilization Act and the later Gradual Enfranchisement Act. Claims of alcohol abuse could be used by the Superintendent General of Indian Affairs to strip

---

[178] Kuokkanen, *Restructuring Relations*, 2; 12. See also Deer, *Beginning and End of Rape*.
[179] Defriend and Cook, "Reawakening of Indigenous"; Lawrence, "Gender, Race, and Regulation."
[180] For discussion of these myths in Australia, see d'Abbs and Hewlett, "Explaining Aboriginal Alcohol Use."

someone of the very basic benefits accruing to them by virtue of being Indigenous. Métis journalist Chelsea Vowel identifies a three-stage process: alcohol was intentionally introduced by white traders and settlers. It was then banned due to claims that Indigenous Peoples were genetically prone to alcoholism. Any alcohol consumption was classified by the state as "abuse," even if considerably less was consumed than in settler homes. Severe penalties were allocated against Indigenous Peoples, which included the removal of children, denial of rations, and sometimes imprisonment.[181]

Claims of Indigenous alcoholism were widespread in official government documents, especially in annual reports by Indian Affairs; this theme remained consistent over time. In 1880, Superintendent General Edgar Dewdney observed: "The effect upon Indians generally of the immoderate use of ardent spirits is to render them frenzied – they completely lose their self-control." Spirits, he argued, "arouse in him his savage nature afresh, and to lead him to the commission of the most fiendish crimes."[182] By 1898, James Smart, Deputy Superintendent General, noted a decline in what he called "the drinking class," with the rise of temperance on reserves. However, there were still dangers, and "liquor, if indulged in at all, provoke[s] a far stronger craving in an Indian than in an ordinary white man," and will "render him reckless as to the cost at which he gratifies the passion when excited."[183]

In 1907, Frank Pedley, Deputy Superintendent General, echoed similar views, noting: "there is no one vice so dangerous to Indians as that of indulgence in strong drink, for not only are they peculiarly predisposed by temperament to such indulgence, but they lack the stamina of constitution which enables white men longer to resist its deleterious action, and when under its immediate influence they more completely lose control of themselves in all directions." The myth of alcoholism was often coupled with the belief in redemption through Christianity and missionary activity. For Pedley, conditions had improved, largely due to the work of Indian agents, supported by "the sympathy of the great majority of the Indians, who themselves recognize the danger to their race." However, he primarily applauded "the missionaries of the gospel who labour among them [and] deserve much of the credit."[184]

As with government publications, school textbooks and general histories echoed the same mythology, including a stock morality play that pitted Indigenous Peoples as victims against selfish traders (the bad white men) versus the good white men from the government and the missions. For many settlers, conversion was one of the best antidotes to the problems supposedly plaguing

---

[181] Vowel, *Indigenous Writes*. [182] Canada, "Annual Report 1889," xiv.
[183] Canada, "Annual Report 1897," xxx. [184] Canada, "Annual Report 1907," xxiv.

Indigenous communities. Christianity and European civilization were presented as more egalitarian and democratic than traditional Indigenous societies, and more suited to cope with the rapidly changing world. David Duncan's 1908 history of the Prairie provinces extolled the "Jesuit missionaries," who risked "their lives and endured great hardships in order to bring the Christian religion to the Indians and train them in habits that would make them more happy and more healthy." He compared these to the fur traders who, by contrast, sought wealth at the expense of the "ignorant Indians" by encouraging "fire-water."[185] Percy Evans (1914) credited the missionaries and their "noble work" in "dealing with these degenerate descendants of a once mighty and noble race."[186] He echoed Duncan's praise of the labours of Jesuit missionaries, for being "one of the noblest annals in the history of the world," braving "untold dangers and miseries" to spread the gospel.[187]

Others, however, noted that Christians should do more, lamenting how many Christian settlers were too passive in the face of the whiskey trade. Mellick for example (1909) articulated: "The bad white man gives him the black drink, and the Christian white man stands by and sees the helpless Indian debased and robbed of all that is left to him worth possessing and does little to protect or help him." It was therefore the role of the "good" white man to intervene.[188] Mellick regretted the lost opportunity to use goodness to promote full assimilation. Had Indians been "treated in a truly Christian manner and had a Christian example being set before them, they would be 'White Indians' today, or at least measure well up to the standard of good Christian citizens."[189]

Thompson Ferrier, Methodist minister and former Principal of the Brandon Indian Residential School in the province of Manitoba, conveyed a similar theme in his 1912 book, noting how "the white man's vices have taken a deeper root than his virtues. His fire-water and the diseases he has introduced have demoralized whole tribes."[190] Weaver's 1919 school textbook echoed a similar theme of an Indigenous problem with "fire-water": "When once the passion for drink seized them they would part with all they had to obtain it. Some even sold their children for the sake of getting 'French milk' as they called it."[191]

Louis Norman Tucker's 1914 appeal to "protect the native races" included gratitude to the Indians for allowing settlers to "inherit ... this magnificent Dominion." What follows is a typical *mea culpa*: "We have destroyed their

---

[185] Duncan, "Prairie Provinces," 14–15.   [186] Evans, "History of the Prairie Provinces," 34.
[187] Evans, "History of the Prairie Provinces," 14.
[188] Mellick, *Indians and Our Indian Missions*, 42–43.
[189] Mellick, *Indians and Our Indian Missions*, 4–5.   [190] Ferrier, *Our Indians*.
[191] Weaver, *A Canadian History*, 39.

hunting-grounds and taken their livelihood from them. We have decimated them with our diseases and our fire water, and degraded them with our vices." The solution however lay in more and better British civilization, not less, to encourage quicker adaption to settler ways. Citizenship was one obvious solution, and Tucker also cited approvingly the "splendid instruments" possessed by the state, including the Reserves, and "the complete system of Boarding, Residential and Industrial Schools."[192]

Weaving patriotism into this too, Canada was presented as the positive Indigenous-friendly nation protecting them from the evils of the American whiskey trade. In overtly racist language, Evans blamed illicit American traders for "rapidly reducing the Redskins into a liquor sodden race of degenerates, quarrelsome, dangerous, and useless." He concluded: "Apparently the whiskey bottle was fast becoming the God of the Indian, and the 'blessings' of civilization were being poured down his throat instead of being instilled into his brain." Evans' goal, it seems, was to justify the expansion of European settlement, especially the permanent presence of the Northwest Mounted Police, to, as he puts it "supervise the Indian tribes and to stamp out the nefarious practice of supplying the Redskins with strong drink."[193]

By 1961 the tone of commentary around claims of Indigenous alcoholism had changed, but the underlying assumptions behind the myth remained. A reference paper from the Department of Citizenship and Immigration noted of Indigenous Peoples: "Liquor has presented a special problem." As such, the government: "thought necessary to control the liquor traffic with Indians," through special legislation prohibiting the sale and consumption of alcohol "except for medicinal purposes."[194]

Refuting the Alcoholism Myth and the Need for Christian Conversion

It has been clear for many decades that there is simply no genetic basis for alcoholism amongst Indigenous Peoples, who can metabolize alcohol as well as Europeans. Members of both groups have a high probability of sharing the same seven genes which help create enzymes that break down alcohol (namely: alcohol dehydrogenase and aldehyde dehydrogenase). As Vowel articulates, any problems with alcohol have been dependent on factors which all people share: "genetics, age, social norms and laws, social involvement, economics, mental health, emotional pain or trauma, self-esteem, and environment."[195] Also important to note is that in Canada, First Nations adults currently have

---

[192] Tucker, *Protection of Native Races*. [193] Evans, "History of the Prairie Provinces," 38–39.
[194] Canada, "Canadian-Indian," 2. [195] Vowel, *Indigenous Writes*.

a greater tendency than non-Indigenous Peoples to abstain from alcohol, with abstinence rates at over 34 percent.[196] In an older piece for CBC, Saskatchewan Treaty Commissioner[197] Kathy Walker discussed problems of alcohol and drug dependence amongst some Indigenous Peoples, but noted that the root causes had been known for some times: "residential schools, the Indian Act, child welfare issues, Indian agents, geographic isolation, racism, intergenerational trauma – the list goes on."[198]

The settler myth of Indigenous alcoholism has resulted in harmful views which are damaging to Indigenous health, especially when health care institutions choose to deny or delay treatment based on prejudice.[199] A study from 2019 described how doctors often blame Indigenous Peoples if they have negative health status. An ignorance of the social determinants of health can lead to an institutional culture of blaming Indigenous Peoples, provoking stigma.[200]

The promotion of Christian conversion was intimately tied up with myths of alcoholism. The work of the TRC and the OISI both demonstrate the widespread destruction caused by Christian churches to Indigenous individuals, communities, and nations. Far from helping Indigenous Peoples, missionaries and church officials and the institutions they ran undermined their sovereignty and well-being.[201] The destructive work of missionaries has been discussed for some time. In a 1973 publication, the National Indian Brotherhood (the precursor to the Assembly of First Nations) laid out the extent of damage to Indigenous communities:

> Regarding us as utter and contemptible savages, ... missionaries sought to convert us not only to European religious tenets, but also to European notions of 'property' and 'work.' Missionaries popularized the view that we were obtuse and lazy merely because [we] were reluctant to forgo our integral relation with our environment and adopt the European agricultural industrial property and work ethic.[202]

There is insufficient space here to revisit the harms caused by the forcible assimilation of Indigenous Peoples through conversion, the IRS system, and the day schools. Religious leaders encouraged the outlawing of Indigenous spiritual practices and the literal demonization of Indigenous Peoples who did

---

[196] Vowel, *Indigenous Writes*.
[197] The role involves monitoring the status of the numbered treaties within the provincial borders of Saskatchewan.
[198] Vowel, *Indigenous Writes*. [199] McLane et al., "Impacts of Racism," 5–6.
[200] Wylie and McConkey, "Insiders' Insight," 42. [201] MacDonald, "Match and Exceed."
[202] National Indian Brotherhood, "Aboriginal People," 3.

not wish to adopt Christianity. The author provides detailed analysis in his book *The Sleeping Giant Awakens*.[203]

Myths of Meritocracy and the Liberal Democratic (Racial) State

A number of modern prejudices are based on denigrating Indigenous Peoples for their seeming inability to assimilate into the settler state, which is presented as a neutral container with universally beneficial properties. In his discussions of settler colonialism throughout the CANZUS states, Robert Nichols has developed the term "Settler Contract" to describe "the strategic use of the fiction of a society as the product of a 'contract' between its founding members when it is employed in these historical moments to displace the question of that society's actual formation in acts of conquest, genocide and land appropriation."[204] This is true of all settler states, including Australia, ANZ, and the USA.

Bain Attwood notes the widespread acceptance of simplistic myths that legitimate the nation and largely ignore the violence on which it was founded. These "provid[e] a simple charter for the nation's present and future rather than seeking to understand the past in all its messiness."[205] Absent such acknowledgment, it becomes easier to spread the myth that the settler state is a land of equal opportunity, with everyone having the same life chances, irrespective of Indigeneity, race, gender, or sexuality.

Historical narratives promote the fairness and equality of the Canadian system, which universally rewards personal merits such as hard work, talent, and ingenuity. The established order, despite its inequalities and hierarchies, is legitimate because settlers have earned what they have. Sheelah Mclean (a settler teacher and one of the founders of the Indigenous-led activist movement Idle No More) paraphrases her family's thinking: they gained "social and political status in society through intelligence and hard work alone." There is much obfuscation and denial, however, as racially dominant groups have far more access to resources, opportunities, and power, which have been deliberately denied to Indigenous Peoples and racialized groups. As she explains: "The myth of meritocracy reinforces liberal individualism, providing the public with racist explanations for the vast inequalities that exists between Indigenous people and white settler society."[206]

As Vowel notes however, Canada has never had a level playing field, and historical injustice is not over – there has not been a "magical moment" where

---

[203] MacDonald, *Sleeping Giant*. See also Innes, "Historians and Indigenous Genocide."
[204] Nichols, "Indigeneity," 168.   [205] Attwood, *Telling the Truth*, 14.
[206] Mclean, "We Built a Life," 32.

"contemporary fairness" has replaced centuries of injustice.[207] A staple of settler colonial theory is that the structures established by the state are fundamentally unequal towards Indigenous Peoples. Whether consciously or not, as per Lorenzo Veracini, settlers have "inherited structures of domination that are inherently unjust." This renders settlers complicit in maintaining the structures of settler colonialism. Rather than the system running along parallel lines with forms of Indigenous governance, or excluding them, it was designed to replace them: "Canada as a settler colonial polity was not made without Indigenous peoples, it was made against them."[208] The belief in a Canadian meritocracy remains crucial to this country's appeal; most settlers (even the newest ones) are emotionally invested in this idea. This social contract is simple to grasp: if newcomers work hard, follow the laws and rules, they will reap rewards for themselves, and what they gain can become private property, guaranteed by the state, and then passed along to their descendants in perpetuity.

Early Myths of (Racially Selective) Meritocracy

From its inception, Canada's meritocracy was designed to benefit would-be settlers at the expense of Indigenous Peoples, especially where access to land was concerned.[209] Indigenous Peoples were prohibited by the 1876 Indian Act from homesteading on the Prairies and were confined to a maximum of 160 acres for a family of five (much less for smaller families).[210] As John Tobias explains, the government sought to transform Indigenous Peoples into "imitation Europeans" through the Indian Act and other instruments. Through enfranchisement, they would become citizens, lose their status, and claim a portion of their former reserve as private property, while ultimately full enfranchisement would end the reserve system. To prepare Indigenous Peoples to become citizens within the settler political order, an elected band council system was forced on First Nations. The Superintendent General of Indian Affairs had sweeping powers to lease Indigenous lands for mining, farmland, and for highways and railways, without consent of the First Nations involved.[211]

All of this freed-up land for further colonization. Pre-dating the numbered Treaties, in what would become the Prairie Provinces, the 1872 Dominion Lands Act gave settler heads of household the opportunity to gain 160 acres of free farmland. Racially Anglo-Saxon peoples were privileged by successive ministers of the interior, who sought those who would be a "culturally good fit,"

---

[207] Vowel, *Indigenous Writes*.   [208] Veracini, "Cost of Reconciliation," 81.
[209] See Starblanket and Hunt, *Storying Violence*, Chapter 1, for an overview of this myth, complete with early boosterist posters. They also signal its highly gendered and heteronormative aspects.
[210] Moss and Gardner-O'Toole, *Aboriginal People*.
[211] Tobias, "Protection, Civilization, Assimilation," 205–210.

and of "the right racial backgrounds." These criteria were eventually relaxed to encompass a wider range of Europeans, while people of African and Asian ancestry were deliberately excluded.[212]

Early myths of meritocracy were racially selective and were aimed at a particular type of European who would be able to thrive in the cold weather. Those tasked with writing boosterist literature in the nineteenth century emphasized the opportunities for the right sort of people. Thomas Spence, then Clerk of the Legislative Assembly of Manitoba, wrote a hopeful if racially charged tome in 1879 about the prospects for European settlement:

> The future of citizens of the northwest of Canada will have Norse, Celtic and Saxon blood in his veins. His countenance in the *pure, dry* electric air, will be as fresh as the morning. His muscles will be iron, his nerve steel. Vigor will characterize his very action; for climate gives quality to the blood, strength to the muscles, power to the brain. Indolence is characteristic of people living in the tropics, and energy of those in temperate zones.[213]

Spence praised the "glory" of Canada for purchasing lands to distribute to "the landless of old nations, extending to them a cordial welcome to come and partake of the bounties which the enterprising and industrious may secure." Here was plenty of opportunity for advancement, as long as would-be settlers were willing to work hard and were of the right racial background.[214] The state also promised a stable, honest, meritocratic system, including "British constitutional laws, ample protection to life and property, a healthy climate, and a fertile soil."[215] The desire of advancement for individuals and families was a common theme. For Charles Lucas (1901) British motives for migration to North America was not premised on "the lust of conquest" or the "glamour of adventure," but were instead based on the desire for financial security and the chance for advancement, "of always moving a little further and winning a little more."[216]

By 1914, Prairie settlement has advanced, and networks of towns and cities were established, linked by rail. In a boosterist pamphlet published by the Canadian Ministry of the Interior, the government argued that the restrictive days of settlement only by the "hardy young adventurer" were over. Canada now called "to the settler and to his wife and children." The state could promise not only "larger financial returns, but of domestic happiness in a pure, wholesome environment." As to the goals of government, they argued that land was worth giving away, since "agriculture is the foundation of a progressive

---

[212] Rollings-Magnusson, *Homesteaders*, 4; 13.   [213] Spence, *Prairie Lands*, 6.
[214] Spence, *Prairie Lands*, 9.   [215] Spence, *Prairie Lands*, 50.
[216] Lucas, *Historical Geography*, 44–45.

country." Further, the government defined the typical settler as "Canadians, English, Scotch, Irish, French, and English-speaking Americans (who are going in, in large numbers), with Germans and Scandinavians."[217]

How did Indigenous Peoples fit into this mix? For the state, there was always a two-pronged approach of keeping those deemed racially undesirable out of the country while assimilating those within. Indigenous Peoples would be selectively granted the right to form part of the meritocratic society, but not right away, and only if they deserved it. Gratitude was expected, and resent built when Indigenous Peoples chose not to assimilate and give up their own civilizations. Maclean (1896) in his account of the Mi'kmaq people in the province of Prince Edward Island highlighted a stark contrast between those who chose to assimilate and those who refused. The positive example was "those who stay at home and devote themselves to agriculture, reaping a blessing in comfort, an improved moral sentiment, and the pleasure which arises from industrious habits." This was contrasted with "those who pursue a nomadic life, loitering around the towns in poverty, with little to eat and very poorly clad." These he noted, "especially, are passing away."[218]

Given the passing of Indigenous Peoples, MacLean promoted the merits of civilization and conversion, to "save the man," through training and integration into the settler systems, under the "watchful care of the Government and the churches during his progress from savagery to civilization." Missions and schools would help the younger generations move into agriculture and cattle-raising. The process would take some time and would not be accomplished in a single generation. However, settlers must do their duty, and thereby "some progress toward his ultimate salvation will have been gained."[219]

The collection of myths discussed here created the impression that the landmass now called Canada was a "civilizational vacuum," an empty land, ready and open for European settlement and improvement. Indigenous governments, laws, traditions, and spiritual practices had been discredited, alongside widespread myths about Indigenous characterological defects. The focus for government and for settlers was assimilation into the mainstream. Smart was clear in his 1897 Indian Affairs *Annual Report* that Indigenous self-government was to be discouraged, especially in relation to "the hereditary system," which he argued, "tends to retard the inculcation of that spirit of individuality without which no substantial progress is possible." The focus of his department, as he described it was to "gradually to do away with the hereditary and introduce an elective system, so making (as far as circumstances permit) these chiefs and

---

[217] Canada, "Canada West." [218] Maclean, *Canadian Savage Folk*, 134.
[219] Maclean, *Canadian Savage Folk*, 552.

councillors occupy the position in a band which a municipal council does in a white community."[220]

Missionary views were little different. From a Methodist perspective, Ferrier (1906) advanced individual assimilation as the best way forwards. He put it that "The Indian massed in tribes is the problem. The Indian with individual opportunity is no problem." Individualizing people as "a unit, and hold him responsible as such," he argued, "is the true method of civilizing the Indian." By contrast, federal recognition of Indigenous Peoples, "tends to help the Indian to remain idle, un-progressive, and dependent, and the inevitable result is discontent, lawlessness, unrest, laziness, debauchery, and pauperism." As for the Treaties, these could safely be discarded as counterproductive to Indigenous interests. Indeed: "To be a free man in the enjoyment of life is vastly better than to be bound to an ignorant tribe. Both church and state should have as a final goal the destruction and end of treaty and reservation life."[221] In a later publication from 1912, Ferrier reiterated the perspective:

> I do not believe in Indian rights any more than I do in German rights or Irish rights. There should be no special rights. The Indian has the same right to make a man of himself as the white man. He has the same right to live a decent, honest, and industrious life, to become a good citizen with a clean, moral character, and there his rights end.[222]

Later views from the government were more anodyne but similar. In a publication by the federal government and the Canadian Broadcasting Corporation, Thomas Crerar, federal minister of mines and resources (1937) noted: "we must recognize our moral obligation to help the Indian adjust himself to the vastly changed conditions that we ourselves have brought about. We, the intruders, so to speak, have deprived him of his old mode of living. We have swept it off his feet. In fairness, we should help him to regain them again." Crerar reminded his audience that Indigenous Peoples had only been in contact with European civilization for about a century. It was therefore the position of Canadians "as individuals," to help "the Indian along the path of self-development and progress, by extending to him a kindly sympathy and an understanding of his problem."[223]

The primary goal of a 1963 pamphlet, published by the Royal Canadian Geographical Society, was to make sense from a settler view of how Indigenous Peoples thought. Overt racism was set aside in favour of more coded language: "their ideals and values differ from those of modern business. They are prone to share rather than save. Their life involves bursts of intense activity and

---

[220] Canada, "Annual Report 1898." [221] Ferrier, *Indian Education*, 16.
[222] Ferrier, *Our Indians*, 18. [223] CBC, *Indians Speak to Canada,* 38–39.

occasionally long periods of comparative idleness. It is difficult for them to see the need for, and even harder to follow, the study time clock routine of most industrial work period."[224] The pamphlet followed a familiar narrative in encouraging assimilation as a means of ending the problems of Indigenous deficiency: "much remains to be done by all Canadians before the Indian portion of the population may be said to share fully in the general community's economic and social activities."[225]

Diamond Jenness, one of Canada's most distinguished anthropologists, and reputedly a great admirer of Indigenous Peoples, would predict the end of their separate existence with little regret, seeing assimilation as a positive if inevitable development:

> Doubtless all the tribes will disappear. Some will endure only a few years longer, others, like the Eskimo, may last several centuries. Some will merge steadily with the white race, others will bequeath to future generations only an infinitesimal fraction of their blood. Culturally they have already contributed everything that was valuable for our own civilization beyond what knowledge we may still glean from their histories concerning man's ceaseless struggle to control his environment.[226]

A rhetorical veneer of paternalism for Indigenous Peoples was used to divest them of their lands, which were then given over to European settlement in many cases. Other lands were simply retained as Crown lands and thus taken out of Indigenous hands. Some discourses of reconciliation have focused on equality and meritocracy as methods by which to redress past abuses. Indigenous Peoples deserved to be equal to settler Canadians in terms of their access to water, housing, employment, healthcare, and education. In a previous publication, I have employed the term "soft reconciliation," reflecting Anishinaabe political scientist Sheryl Lightfoot's analysis of "soft Indigenous rights." These include collective rights to language, culture, spiritual beliefs and practices, educational systems, and other forms of identity. These are perceived as extensions of current human rights norms and practices, and while they may impose some obligations, these can be met largely within the existing structures of the settler state.[227] Soft reconciliation is more palatable to settlers because it reaffirms the largesse of the Canadian state, filling gaps and "bringing up" Indigenous Peoples to a settler standard.

By contrast hard rights, and by extension "hard reconciliation," are more difficult for the settler state to enact in terms of cost and effort. These are also

---

[224] Dunstan, *Canadian Indians Today*, 6.   [225] Dunstan, *Canadian Indians Today*, 15.
[226] Jenness, *Indians of Canada*, 264.
[227] Lightfoot, *Global Indigenous Politics*, 29–30. MacDonald, "Paved with Comfortable Intentions."

existentially harder because to recognize their necessity is to concede that the state is based on a legal fiction, and that the Crown does not own the land over which it asserts control. Hard rights, as Lightfoot explains, are exemplified by "self-determination and land rights for Indigenous nations, with or without statehood," and are therefore less commensurable with the current structures of the settler state. Potentially, "state territorial sovereignty" is under question when issues of hard rights are raised.[228] A key focus of the resurgence of Indigenous rights has been a desire for the return of stolen lands.

Soft rights and soft reconciliation are both closely tied to myths of the meritocratic state. The federal government has promoted such mythology for a very long time, and it continues still in the 2021 edition of *Discover Canada*, which promotes a strong assimilatory agenda for newcomers into a very positively presented state. Canada is celebrated as "a strong and free country," with a "unique identity," and "the oldest continuous constitutional tradition in the world."[229] In their section on "Citizenship Responsibilities," they are clear that "Obeying the law" is crucial to being Canadian, alongside "[t]aking responsibility for oneself and one's family – Getting a job, taking care of one's family and working hard in keeping with one's abilities are important Canadian values."[230] To be Canadian means to be a worker and contribute; meritocratic principles undergird settler society: "A belief in ordered liberty, enterprise, hard work and fair play has enabled Canadians to build a prosperous society in a rugged environment..."[231]

Recent survey data indicates that a large proportion of Canadians support these positions. Angus Reid polling from 2023 demonstrates an overwhelming support for meritocracy: with 59 percent believing hard work, 58 percent believing level of education, 51 percent believing personal ambition, and 39 percent believing good social skills were central to success. By contrast, much smaller percentages believe that non-meritocratic factors impede getting ahead, such as: class (7 percent); race or ethnicity (8 percent); and gender (6 percent).[232]

Myths of Meritocracy and Multiculturalism: The Colour-Blind Society

As Canada changes demographically, and more racialized newcomers immigrate, multiculturalism and tolerance for diversity allows the country to be more welcoming. However, multiculturalism can also dilute Indigenous rights, to

---

[228] Lightfoot, *Global Indigenous Politics*, 29–30. MacDonald, "Paved with Comfortable Intentions."
[229] Canada, *Discover Canada*. [230] Canada, *Discover Canada*.
[231] Canada, *Discover Canada*. [232] Angus Reid, "Canadians & Class."

promote soft cultural rights at the expense of implementing hard rights. Multicultural models can purportedly accommodate Indigenous Peoples, promoting a social and economic contract whereby anyone who is willing to contribute to Canadian society can belong. This view is not new. Paul Chartrand has noted a "strong public perception that views Aboriginal peoples as historically disadvantaged racial minorities rather than distinct societies of an inherently political nature, societies which are relevant political communities entitled to participate in crafting a legitimate political order."[233]

The history and ongoing practices of settler colonialism are largely erased from view. Again, *Discover Canada* offers a contemporary interpretation, proudly claiming that the country is a "land of immigrants" since, over the past two centuries, "millions of newcomers have helped to build and defend our way of life. Many ethnic and religious groups live and work in peace as proud Canadians."[234] Canada is seen as a society not based on dominant races, cultures, or languages, but potentially open to embracing all peoples. The structural elements of the state, especially its institutions, are not recognized as being settler colonial, British and French, but rather as having universal merit.[235] A 2019 Environics survey indicated that a large proportion of respondents felt that Indigenous rights were not distinctive and that an equality paradigm should inform government decision-making: "48 percent see Indigenous Peoples as being just like other cultural or ethnic groups in Canada's multicultural society, while 42 percent see them as having unique rights as the first inhabitants of the continent."[236]

Early myths of meritocracy conveniently elided the strongly racially biased decisions about who could enter Canada and who was denied. Restrictive "White Canada" immigration policies targeted Asians and South Asians in particular, and immigration policies were designed to encourage more white Europeans to become settlers. Prime Minister William Lyon Mackenzie King famously sought to exclude Asian immigrants on the premise that they would "change the fundamental composition of the Canadian population." Later decision-makers would couch the policies in terms of attracting "immigrants from countries with political and social institutions similar to our own" to quote Jack Pickersgill, MacKenzie King's Minister of Citizenship and Immigration.[237]

In 1947, the Liberal government of Prime Minister Louis St Laurent created the Department of Citizenship and Immigration (merging the Nationalities Branch and Indian Affairs), with the goal, as St Laurent put it, of making "Canadian citizens of those who come here as immigrants and to make

---

[233] Chartrand, "Self-Determination," 303. [234] Canada, *Discover Canada*.
[235] Sharma, "Canadian Multiculturalism," 86. [236] Environics, "Towards Reconciliation," 9.
[237] Ellermann, *Comparative Politics of Immigration*, 195–196.

Canadian citizens of as many as possible of the descendants of the original inhabitants of this country." In both cases, the new Department focused on assimilating non-Europeans. To this end they created a targeted publication for Indigenous Peoples (*Indian News*) promoting individual achievement and assimilation as the path to success.[238]

During the 1960s, widespread demographic changes presaged demands for a broader less rigidly British-centred national identity. In 1969, the Royal Commission on Bilingualism and Biculturalism recommended the integration rather than the assimilation of non-British ethnic groups.[239] Canadian Prime Minister Pierre Trudeau, in his *White Paper* laid out a vision where Indigenous Peoples would be "made" the same as every other Canadian. Trudeau, with then Indian Affairs Minister (later Prime Minister) Jean Chretien, sought to end the existence of Indigenous Peoples as a "race apart." Trudeau suggested that reserves were akin to "ghettoes," and cast doubt on the legitimacy of Indigenous "ancestral rights" in a modern Western country. Treaties were presented as antiquated, and Trudeau declared his desire that Indigenous Peoples "should become Canadians as all other Canadians."[240]

The *White Paper* would have brought unilateral abrogation of the treaties, and thus provoked strong reactions within Indigenous communities, who rose up and derailed the initiative. As Dale Turner (Temagami First Nation) has articulated, "White Paper liberalism" was consistent with Western European political ideals, which privileged the individual as the central unit of a political system, while seeking primarily to balance both the freedom and equality of individuals operating in the society.[241] For many Indigenous Peoples, the Multiculturalism Act in 1971 was closely tied to the same vision represented by the *White Paper*. Both represented a desire to assimilate non-Europeans into settler society. When introducing both multiculturalism and bilingualism to the House of Commons in 1971, Trudeau articulated that while Canada had two official languages, there was no dominant culture or ethnicity or as it put it, "No citizen or group of citizens is other than Canadian, and all should be treated fairly."[242] This effectively elided the dominant British and French nature of Canadian culture, language, laws, and institutions.

Some contemporary multiculturalism theorists have also promoted the immigrant identity of Canada, while tacitly recognizing but also downplaying the importance of Indigenous Peoples. As the seminal multicultural theorist Will Kymlicka has stated: "Canada has largely been built by settlers and immigrants who have left the constraints of the old world behind, to start a new life in a new

---

[238] Hayward, *Identity and Industry*, 95–96.
[239] Dewing and Leman, "Canadian Multiculturalism." [240] Borrows, "Re-Living," 103–104.
[241] Turner, *Not a Peace Pipe*, 13. [242] Trudeau, "Canadian Culture."

land." While he inserts a caveat that "Canada was not a *terra nullius*," he is nevertheless content to advance a view of Canada as "a young, modern society, free from the old hierarchies, cultural prejudices and embedded traditions of the Old World. It is, Canadians like to think, a classless, meritocratic and democratic society, open to newcomers and to new ideas."[243]

Such views are problematic for Indigenous rights. Vowel describes multiculturalism as creating the conditions whereby Indigenous Peoples "exist as Canadians and celebrate surface culture (food/music/clothing) without existing as a separate legal category. Indigenous peoples would need to stop advancing their claims to Indigenous rights, and exist within a framework of Canadian rights." However: "Giving that up to become Canadian and to be folded into a Western liberal-rights framework is the definition of assimilation."[244] Rachel George, a Nuučaańuł political scientist, notes how narratives of multicultural tolerance can "divest Indigeneity from Indigenous communities, consuming it as Canada's multicultural identity, and effectively extinguishing Indigenous nationhood'. In other words, "Inclusion is just the Canadian word for assimilation."[245]

Some immigrants may relate to Indigenous Peoples as fellow victims of a colonial system, for example, the Japanese internments and Chinese head taxes were highly discriminatory. While this shared marginalization may build bridges of empathy, it does not imply equality or sameness. Indeed, racialized peoples have sometimes become part of the problem. In a seminal article, Bonita Lawrence and Ena Dua highlighted the exclusion of Indigenous Peoples and perspectives within antiracism movements. After all: "Histories of the settlement of people of color have been framed by racist exclusion and fail to account for the ways in which their settlement has taken place on Indigenous land."[246] Sunera Thobani has highlighted similar dynamics, describing: "The more immigrants have sought their own inclusion and access to citizenship, the more invested they have become, with very few exceptions, in supporting the nation's erasure of its originary violence and its fantasies of progress and prosperity."[247]

This does not preclude mutual understanding and alliance building, and Indigenous and Black scholars have drawn parallels as well as distinctions between their communities, when faced with five centuries of colonization and alienation from ancestral lands and cultures.[248] A recent publication by Leanne Simpson and Robyn Maynard outlines the shared struggles and vibrancies of both peoples in resisting white domination, settler colonialism, and

---

[243] Kymlicka, "Being Canadian," 175. [244] Vowel, *Indigenous Writes*.
[245] George, "Inclusion." [246] Lawrence and Dua, "Decolonizing Anti-Racism," 134.
[247] Thobani, *Exalted Subjects*, 16. [248] Simpson, et al., "An Exchange," 76.

capitalism.[249] The focus is on bridge building against common challenges, although there is also recognition that Indigenous rights are different, based on distinct claims to territory and nationhood.[250] The argument here is that meritocracy along European settler lines creates a particular framework into which non-Europeans and Indigenous Peoples are expected to fit.

Québec and Indigenous Peoples: Distinctive Relations and Myths

This final section focuses on myths about Indigenous Peoples in the province of Québec. Québec has a distinct history from the rest of Canada, being comprised primarily of territory that was settled and later colonized by France, which did not sign treaties with Indigenous nations. Québec has maintained a civil (rather than common) law tradition, and is predominantly French-speaking. Québec promotes interculturalism rather than multiculturalism, which privileges integration into a French linguistic and cultural environment, which is deemed to be under threat in a predominantly Anglophone continent. Much of their mythology about Indigenous Peoples has its own particular characteristics. The distinctive nature of settler colonialism in Québec means that some studies of Indigenous-settler relations often draw distinctions between this province and the rest of Canada.[251]

The British colonial system may have precipitated some of the conflict between French settlers and Indigenous Peoples. For example, the 1763 Royal Proclamation and the Québec Act worked together to recognize and affirm some rights of autonomy and self-government for Indigenous Peoples, with some land rights. However, the Proclamation was primarily designed to spread British law and government, and reduce French influence, with the goal of submerging French speakers, as well as limiting Roman Catholicism. The British, as Eva Mackey explains, effectively "played different populations against each other in the interests of the British colonial project, paradoxically giving Native peoples land rights in order to control and assimilate members of another European culture."[252]

English-French biculturalism has been based on a compact theory of Canadian politics, as an official Québec government publication explains,

---

[249] Maynard and Simpson, *Rehearsals for Living*, 24; 29. They argue: "Imperialism and ongoing colonialism have been ending worlds for as long as they have been in existence, and Indigenous and Black peoples have been building worlds and then rebuilding worlds for as long as we have been in existence." 46.
[250] Simpson, *Mohawk Interruptus*, 16.
[251] For example, the National Inquiry into Missing and Murdered Indigenous Women and Girls (2019) featured a separate report on Quebec.
[252] Mackey, *House of Difference*, 27.

a "compact between free and autonomous provinces ... [not] a mere creation of the imperial [British] Parliament."[253] This ideal is complicated by the prior existence of Indigenous nations, possessed of their own territories, governments, worldviews, and practices, who demonstrate the problematic nature of some French settler-Canadians seeking to embrace a form of ersatz indigeneity.

Québec has been the locus of its own "emancipatory nationalism," due to a sense of French settler political and cultural alienation within the federal state. This was certainly true historically, although now, in the era of a Coalition Avenir Québec government, the sense of resentment and anger has dissipated somewhat.[254] The concept of Québec as a nation predates their military defeat at the hands of the British. Nationalism can be understood as a movement closely associated with historical writing and the rise of academic historiography during the global nineteenth century. The Parti Nationale was created by Honoré Mercier in 1885, and later, the Union Nationale was formed in 1935. The name of the provincial legislature would be changed to L'Assemblée nationale in 1968.[255] All of this differentiates Québec from any other Canadian province (despite weak analogues in Alberta's periodic calls for independence) and changes the nature of Indigenous-settler relations to one of contesting historical, cultural, and territorial nationalisms.

In 1985, the Québec legislature recognized ten Indigenous nations (an eleventh would later follow). However, no specific rights were affirmed through this process. The Québec government's position was that no written treaties were signed with Indigenous Peoples during French rule, and when New France was defeated, no Indigenous rights survived. This theory has animated Québec nationalism. While some Indigenous concerns are recognized as legitimate, any problems are seen to be fully resolvable by Québec through its own distinct political and legal institutions.[256] Not unlike the rest of Canada, successive provincial governments, as well as Québec society in general, have been loath to recognize Québecois as a settler nation that has been complicit in a long history of colonization and subjugation of Indigenous Peoples.[257]

Early Québec historical accounts tended to focus on conflict between the French and Indigenous Peoples. Nineteenth century accounts were similar to those in English Canada – focused on Indigenous Peoples as "savages." As Cecilia Morgan paraphrases in her historiographic analysis: Indigenous Peoples in these accounts were "noted for their warlike tendencies, treachery, cruelty, superstitious nature, and lack of social order and discipline." Only the Hurons,

---

[253] Québec, *Our Way of Being Canadian*, 19.
[254] Salée, "New Face of Québec Nationalism," 122–213.
[255] Castro-Rea, "La Nation, C'est Moi," 67.   [256] Walters, "Constitutive Power," 167; 169.
[257] Laxer, *Unveiling the Nation*, 9.

allied to the French, were seen in a positive light. Historical accounts used Indigenous Peoples as a foil for French Canadian nationalism, from the nineteenth and into the twentieth century.[258] Highly influential until the 1940s were the writings of Lionel Groulx, who promoted a conservative brand of Catholic, rural, French nationalism, strongly critical of immigration, industrialization, English Canada, and democracy. There was also an undercurrent of anti-Semitism in his work.[259]

Québec myths share some commonalities with those in other provinces. Themes of Indigenous Peoples as superstitious, immoral, warlike, and treacherous were common in the standard textbook, *Histoire du Canada*, used in most of Québec's high school history classes. Written by Paul-Emile Farley and Gustave Lamarche, this was reproduced in multiple editions from 1934 into the 1960s. Some textbooks erred in another way, simply erasing an Indigenous presence from the history of Québec. Morgan specifically cites the work of Jean Bruchési and Albert Tessier as typical examples in the 1940s and 1950s. Another theme developed in post-1945 history textbooks – that of Indigenous Peoples as helpful and obliging towards the French in guiding them through the territory, and helping them secure food supplies and local technology for their survival. However, this theme of Indigenous helpers did not extend towards recognizing their many thousands of years of history, nor their deep and abiding claims to ancestral territory.[260]

Indigenous Peoples as Subnational Entities within Québec

While there are frequent changes in governing party, certain myths about Québec as a nation with special rights continue, nevertheless. Bill 99, passed in 2000 by the Parti Québécois government remains law and outlines the rights of a sovereign Québec "state" and its dependent Indigenous nations. As such: "the Québec people, in the majority French-speaking, possesses specific characteristics and a deep-rooted historical continuity in a territory over which it exercises its rights through a modern national state." This includes the right of "the Québec people" to "take charge of its own destiny, determine its political status and pursue its economic, social and cultural development." Indigenous nations are tacitly seen as subnational entities, subordinate to and recognized as existing "within Québec." Similarly, "their right to autonomy within Québec," is based on provincial government recognition.[261]

---

[258] Morgan, *Commemorating Canada*, 161.   [259] Rudin, *Making History*, 16–17.
[260] Morgan, *Commemorating Canada*, 162.
[261] Québec, "Act Respecting Fundamental Rights."

Indigenous Peoples figure as a precursor to Québec nationhood, but not as an impediment to it. The narrative of Indigenous helpers and passers of the sovereignty torch to French Canadians continued during under the provincial Liberal government (generally been seen as less nationalistic and more pro-federalist). Their 2017 publication *Our Way of Being Canadian* submerged a "nation to nation" relationship within a narrative of the French-speaking nation as worthy of extensive recognition and rights to self-preservation. The account of when Europeans "discovered" North America acknowledged that "First Nations had already been living there for millennia," and were "already present in all sectors." The government would recognize Indigenous Peoples as useful helpers for the French, in that they "would prove vital to ambitious exploration expeditions" and "the sharing of respective know-how."[262] While paying lip service to Indigenous Peoples, then Liberal Premier Philippe Couillard was clear that "[o]ur nation is, first and foremost, French-speaking," although he added that it had "been enriched by the diversity and historic contribution of the First Nations and the Inuit, and by English-speaking Québecers."[263]

The more conservative-leaning Coalition Avenir Québec government took power in 2018, continuing similar themes. Their 2022 action plan, "Ensemble," portrays Indigenous Peoples as being specifically tied to Québec ("Les nations autochtones du Québec") viewing them as citizens of Québec and as political and sociological nations.[264] However, in practice the government has had little interest in Indigenous self-determination. For example, in 2025, the CAQ government passed Bill 84, "An Act Respecting National Integration." Embedded within the Bill, in addition to a strong assertion of French Québecois nationhood, was a heavily diluted recognition of Indigenous rights. For example, the Bill is clear that "Québec is a national State, the only French-speaking State in North America, a democratic State, sovereign in its areas of jurisdiction and endowed with the means to guarantee its territorial integrity, which possesses the right to self-determination ... " By contrast, Indigenous Peoples are accorded fewer rights, namely, that as "descendants of the first inhabitants of this land" they have the right "to preserve and develop their original language and culture."[265] Self-determination is not mentioned here.

In 2024, the CAQ government announced the creation of a new "Musée national de l'histoire du Québec," set to open in 2026. Québec Premier François Legault articulated a specific periodization of Québecois national identity, beginning especially with Samuel de Champlain, "who was the founder of

---

[262] Québec, *Our Way of Being Canadian*, 5–6. [263] Québec, *Our Way of Being Canadian*.
[264] Québec, "Ensemble." [265] Québec, "Bill 84," 5.

our nation." This in his view did not deny the existence of Indigenous Peoples but made the point that their prior presence is largely irrelevant to the specific historical narrative his government wants to promote. He recognized the 11 Indigenous nations in Québec but argued that their downplaying in the museum was reasonable. In his logic: "The idea is to show the history of the nation that was French-Canadian and now Québécois, that started with Champlain." He also pledged to "highlight the presence of Indigenous nations who were here before us and who helped us over the years."[266] For Legault, this was acceptable because the Museum is devoted to French Canadians, so there is no need to consult First Nations.[267]

For his part, Assembly of First Nations Québec-Labrador Chief Ghislain Picard noted that Indigenous Peoples were little more than an "afterthought" in the Museum's creation, and that members of his Assembly (which represent the interests of Québec First Nations) were not invited to be represented as experts on the advisory committee when planning the content.[268] Such a response shows the key role of Québec nationalism at the core of power.

Part of this may have to do with the belief amongst some Québecois that Indigenous Peoples have been used as leverage by the federal government to undermine Québec nationalism. Julian Castro-Rea (2005) has traced the origins of this myth to at least the Oka crisis. He charts its popularity during the run up to the 1995 Québec referendum on independence from the rest of Canada, and specifically highlights how Indigenous Peoples who speak English are marshalled as proof that they are both pro-Canadian and anti-Québec. The reality is different – the lack of coherent Québec recognition of Indigenous rights to self-determination and control over their own affairs arguably has a much greater role to play.[269]

Québec as a Victim Nation

Another influential myth in Québec concerns how relatively fair and just were early French settlers when compared to the English / British. Earlier conceptions of French colonial policy and their *mission civilisatrice*, designed to convert and assimilate Indigenous peoples, have been largely downplayed in favour of more positive narratives. This has much to do with the fact that French Canada was colonized by the British, while simultaneously colonizing Indigenous Peoples and lands.[270] This allows Québecois to claim a sort of

---

[266] Lowrie, "Indigenous Criticism." [267] Lalonde, "Systematic Erasure."
[268] Lowrie, "Historians, First Nations leader." [269] Castro-Rea, "La Nation, C'est Moi," 69.
[270] Leroux, *Paradoxes of Race,* 54–55.

moral capital, to be expended against Anglo-Canada but also deployed to delegitimate Indigenous nations within the territorial boundaries of Québec.

However, Québec is not a nation indigenous to North America, nor does it exist separate from its European past. Equally, it does not have a long history on the territory it claims, as do European nations like the Basques, Catalans, or Scottish, to whom they are often compared. In practice, Québec was both a French settler colony in its own right, and later a colonized subject population following their defeat by the British in 1759. Daniel Leroux traces three historical periods in what he terms the myth of "double-colonization." The first is a French dominated settler colonial project, from the seventeenth and eighteenth centuries, followed by subjection after 1763 and until Confederation, after which we see different conceptions of who is in control. A constant theme throughout is the existence of white supremacy, with French settlers moving up and down a racial hierarchy which includes periods of dominance, submergence, and dominance again.[271]

Leroux here raises a crucial point about settler identity and responsibility, noting that French descendants have been raised with a myth of being primarily victims of British colonization. The fact that their French ancestors occupied and colonized large proportions of Canada and the United States for a century and half is rarely discussed, nor is the enslavement of Indigenous Peoples and Africans during this time. The French colonies were connected through broader economic policies which benefited from the interlinked trade in enslaved Africans and sugar.[272]

A certain aesthetic took root amongst the French Québecois intelligentsia in the 1960s, who wholeheartedly embraced the decolonial theories of Frantz Fanon, Aimé Césaire, and Albert Memmi, and claimed to be part of a comparable liberation struggle. Julie Burelle highlights the French Québécois' "often uncritical alignment with racialized and colonized Others and their careful forgetting of their ongoing role as settlers vis-à-vis Indigenous people."[273] This is problematic precisely because, unlike Indigenous Peoples and Black people, French Canadians clearly benefited from whiteness, as a settler population, with ties to Europe, a dominant structural positioning, and the ability to establish colonizing institutions.[274]

This myth of victimhood is easily operationalized, especially against racialized immigrants who are not Francophone, white, or Catholic. The denial of settler colonialism and racism in the case of Québec is troubling, and nationalists frequently deploy immigrants and racialized peoples as "foils for Québec

---

[271] Leroux, "Many Paradoxes," 55. [272] Leroux, *Distorted Descent*, 220.
[273] Burelle, "Critical Distance," 270. [274] Benhadjoudja, "Racial Secularism," 191.

sovereignty or threats to the survival of the French identity."[275] Leila Benhadjoudja discusses the situation as a battle between "two white supremacies," with immigrants "invited to submit to one of the two supremacies, either through the politics of multiculturalism in Canada or through a francophone national identity in Québec."[276]

Myth of an Indigenous "Métis" Nation

Tied to this range of myths is a less popular but nevertheless influential belief that most French Canadians have some Indigenous ancestry, and therefore can claim to be Indigenous if they choose. This myth legitimates the Québec demand for the preservation of French culture and tradition, and its obligations on newcomers to assimilate into its dominant culture and society. It can and has also been used to delegitimate self-determining rights of Indigenous Peoples within the territory of Québec.

Former Québec Minister of Cultural Affairs Denis Vaugeois invoked the concept of a "nation métissé" or a mixed nation, in part to refute and dilute specific First Nations' rights to land and autonomy, based on the argument that all French Canadians could claim Indigenous heritage and thus Indigenous rights. Similarly, legal studies academic Sébastien Malette has sought to merge Québecois and Métis identities as the same, with both "bath[ed] in a historically mixed society and carr[ying] a distinct culture from this fact."[277] Yet, as Leroux notes, claims to Indigenous ancestry rest on weak foundations, where one Indigenous ancestor is claimed from about 300 – 375 years ago, one of a potential 2,000 ancestors through 12 generations.[278] Buttressing Leroux, a 2023 scientific study employed a detailed methodology to evaluate "the degree of the identity-by-descent between Québec individuals and Native American populations." The authors draw the conclusion that "the Québec population is not different from other New World populations of European descent in being enriched in alleles of Native American origin, although the extent of admixture is much lower than in Central and South American populations."[279]

It is instructive that the number of intermarriages, contrary to these myths, were relatively small. Few Indigenous women married French settlers; indeed before 1670 only 12 marriages to Indigenous women are recorded, amongst a population of about 3,700 settlers (primarily men). Leroux demonstrates how false claims of Indigeneity are "used politically to oppose actual, living

---

[275] Livingstone, "Racism versus Culture," 14. [276] Benhadjoudja, "Racial Secularism," 192.
[277] Gaudry and Leroux, "White Settler Revisionism," 121.
[278] Leroux, *Distorted Descent*, 2; 215. [279] Moreau et al., "Native American Admixture," 1–2.

Indigenous peoples." Rather than reflecting on Indigenous ancestry, and returning lands and promoting Indigenous rights to self-determination, the reverse has often been true, and claims of lineal descent are used to counter Indigenous land claims.[280]

French colonial views of Indigenous Peoples in the early seventeenth century, as Leroux discusses, were distinctly racist. Attempts at intermarriage were derived primarily from the desire to Frenchify Indigenous Peoples, and to increase the aggregate French population. The overall goal was to eventually assimilate and eliminate Indigenous Peoples as separate nations and populations.[281] Leroux outlines many of the perils and violence involved in this grand narrative of "friendly cohabitation and mutual respect." What largely disappears from view is the strongly patriarchal nature of French colonization, which sought to subjugate Indigenous women to European norms. In these early myths, French men are seen to be virile and Indigenous women as promiscuous.[282] In the later period after about 1663, intermarriage was frowned on, as French women were brought to the colonies. As Leroux notes, while sexual unions did take place periodically, the mixed-race products of these unions were generally excluded and stigmatized by French colonists and were thus most often raised within Indigenous communities.[283]

These myths in Québec underwrite each other, suggesting a distinctive identity, defined through descent, language, culture, and other attributes, coupled with strong myths of historic victimization and current vulnerability as a cultural and linguistic minority. Indigenous Peoples integrate poorly into the self-conceptions of Québecois and often become subject to discrimination and marginalization, their inherent right to self-determination submerged when the Québecois nation is privileged.

Conclusions: The Lengthy History of History Wars

Theoretically, this Element contextualizes modern history wars within a much longer timeframe, stretching back centuries to early accounts by European explorers and settlers. Rather than locating the inception of these debates to the mid to late twentieth century, I argue instead that the first salvos (such as they were) were fired by European explorers and settlers. Before colonization, Indigenous knowledge systems, governance structures, laws, diplomacy, and trading practices, were flourishing and dominant on the North American continent. The spread of settler colonialism brought with it the development of a wide range of negative myths about Indigenous Peoples and the legitimacy of

---

[280] Leroux, *Distorted Descent*, 2; 215. [281] Leroux, *Distorted Descent*, 10.
[282] Leroux, *Distorted Descent*, 12. [283] Leroux, *Distorted Descent*, 11.

these traditional Indigenous systems were denied. It is thus disingenuous to see the more recent narratives of Indigenous Peoples and their supporters as primarily reactive and radical, seeking to upend a comfortable and mutually beneficial status quo. Rather, these interventions should better be seen as restorative, designed to correct past misperceptions and untruths. Implicit here is a critique of dominant meritocratic principles.

This study has sought to provide a critical analysis of selected myths directed against Indigenous Peoples, which, following the author's argument, have been foundational to the Canadian state, and which have clear echoes in other CANZUS states. Some myths are less salient now than they were when first enunciated in the early or mid-nineteenth century, but all serve political functions, that is: to denigrate the capacity of Indigenous Peoples to exercise their rights to self-determination on their own lands. Through careful analysis, this study has attempted to refute these myths, in the belief that this is a necessary precondition for truth-telling, given their corrosive impact on Indigenous Peoples, and their languages, laws, cultures, governance traditions, and spiritual practices.

It is tempting to focus on bridging gaps, and to use models such as the American Civil rights movement, or multiculturalism, to conceptualize what positive changes for Indigenous Peoples could look like in CANZUS states. However, while these may be well-meaning lenses, they are incomplete, given that Indigenous rights exist in a different category from redress for disadvantaged minority groups. Indigenous rights are guaranteed through treaty and have been fully affirmed through Canada's incorporation of the United Nations Declaration on the Rights of Indigenous Peoples into federal law. The current modern iteration of the history wars can best be seen as a challenge and corrective to dominant settler narratives, Hopefully, this Element can be a contribution to truth-telling, that is: the unpacking and critique of foundational myths to be found not only in Canada, but also in Australia, Aotearoa New Zealand, and the United States.

Bibliography

Allan, Billie, and Janet Smylie, "First Peoples, Second Class Treatment: The Role of Racism in the Health and Well-Being of Indigenous Peoples in Canada," *Wellesley Institute*, 2015, www.wellesleyinstitute.com/wp-content/uploads/2015/02/Summary-First-Peoples-Second-Class-Treatment-Final.pdf.

Amadahy, Zainab, and Bonita Lawrence, "Indigenous Peoples and Black People in Canada: Settlers or Allies?" in Arlo Kempf (ed.), *Breaching the Colonial Contract: Anti-Colonialism in the U.S. and Canada*. Netherlands: Springer, 2009, 105–136.

Anderson, Mark, and Carmen Robertson, *Seeing Red: A History of Natives in Canadian Newspapers*. Winnipeg: University of Manitoba Press, 2011.

Angus Reid Polling, "Truths of reconciliation: Canadians are deeply divided on how best to address Indigenous issues," 2018, https://angusreid.org/indigenous-canada/.

Arneil, Barbara, *John Locke and America: The Defence of English Colonialism*, Oxford: Clarendon Press, 1996.

Assembly of First Nations, "To the Source: Commissioners Report: Assembly of First Nations," Ottawa, ON, 1992.

Attwood, Bain, *Telling the Truth about Aboriginal History*, Crow's Nest: Allen & Unwin, 2005.

Attwood, Bain, and Fiona Magowan, "Introduction," in Bain Attwood and Fiona Magowan (eds.), *Telling Stories Indigenous History and Memory in Australia and New Zealand*. Crows Nest: Allen & Unwin, 2001, xi–1.

Barta, Tony, "A Very British Genocide: Acknowledgement of Indigenous Destruction in the Founding of Australia and New Zealand," in N. Blackhawk, B. Kiernan, B. Madley, and R. Taylor (eds.), *The Cambridge World History of Genocide: Volume II*, Cambridge: Cambridge University Press, 2023, 46–68.

Bartrop, Paul, "The Holocaust, The Aborigines, and The Bureaucracy of Destruction: An Australian Dimension of Genocide," *Journal of Genocide Research* 3, 1 (2001), 75–87.

Baskin, Cyndy, "Systemic Oppression, Violence, and Healing in Indigenous Families and Communities," in Ramona Alaggia, and Cathy Vine (eds.), *Cruel but Not Unusual: Violence in Families in Canada. 3rd ed*. Kitchener Waterloo: Wilfrid Laurier University Press, 2022, 15–48.

Benhadjoudja, Leila, "Racial Secularism as Settler Colonial Sovereignty in Québec," *Islamophobia Studies Journal* 7, 2 (2022), 183–199.

Black, Conrad, "Canada's Treatment of Aboriginals was Shameful but It Was Not Genocide," *National Post*, June 6, 2015. www.nationalpost.com/m/search/blog.html?b=news.nationalpost.com/full-comment/conrad-black-canadas-treatment-of-aboriginals-was-shameful-but-it-was-not-genocide&q=Supreme%20Court&o=1552.

Borrows, John, "The Durability of Terra Nullius: Tsilhqot'in Nation v British Columbia," *University of British Columbia Law Review* 48 (2015), 701–742.

"Ground-Rules: Indigenous Treaties in Canada and New Zealand," *New Zealand Universities Law Review Journal* 22, 2 (2006), 188–212, https://ssrn.com/abstract=2744928.

Recovering Canada: The Resurgence of Indigenous Law. Toronto: University of Toronto Press, 2002.

"Re-Living the Present: Title, Treaties, and the Trickster in British Columbia," *BC Studies* 120 (1998/1999), 99–109. https://doi.org/10.14288/bcs.v0i120.1480.

"Wampum at Niagara: The Royal Proclamation, Canadian Legal History, and Self-Government," in Michael Asch (ed.), *Aboriginal and Treaty Rights in Canada: Essays on Law, Equality, and Respect for Difference.* Vancouver: UBC Press, 1997, 155–172.

Bottici, Chiara, "Rethinking Political Myth, Unpacking the Settler–Colonial Dream of an 'American Arcadia'," *Constellations* 32, 2 (2025), 321–329, https://doi.org/10.1111/1467-8675.12812.

Brantlinger, Patrick, "'Black Armband' versus 'White Blindfold' History in Australia," *Victorian Studies* 46, 4 (2004), 655–674. https://doi.org/10.1353/vic.2005.0003.

Bryce, George, *Short History of the Canadian People.* Toronto: W. J. Gage, 1887.

Burelle, Julie, "Critical Distance: Unsettling Canada from Abroad," in Christopher Kirkey and Richard Nimijean (eds.), *The Construction of Canadian Identity from Abroad.* Singapore: Springer International, 2022.

Byrd, Jodi, *The Transit of Empire: Indigenous Critiques of Colonialism.* Minneapolis: University of Minnesota Press, 2011.

Cairns, Alan, "Coming to Terms with the Past", in John Torpey (ed.), *Politics and the Past: On Repairing Historical Injustices.* Lanham: Rowman & Littlefield, 2003, 77–78.

Catlin, George, *Life among the Indians.* London: Gall and Inglis, 1890.

Canadian Broadcasting Corporation, *The Indians Speak to Canada*. Ottawa: Canadian Broadcasting Corporation / Canadian Department of Indian Affairs / Mines and resources, 1939.

Canel-Çınarbaş, Deniz, and Sophie Yohani, "Indigenous Canadian University Students' Experiences of Microaggressions," *International Journal of Advanced Counselling* 41, 1 (2019), 41–60. https://doi.org/10.1007/s10447-018-9345-z.

Cardinal, Harold, and Walter Hildebrant, *Treaty Elders of Saskatchewan: Our Dream Is that Our Peoples Will One Day Be Clearly Recognized as Nations*. Calgary: University of Calgary Press, 2000.

Cardinal, Harold, *The Unjust Society: The Tragedy of Canada's Indians*. Edmonton: Hurtig, 1969.

Carleton, Sean, Adele Perry, and Omeasoo Wahpasiw, "The Misuse of Indigenous and Canadian History in Colonialism," in Alan Lester (ed.), *The Truth about Empire: Real Histories of the British Empire*. London: Hurst, 2024, 73–92.

Castro-Rea, Julián, "La Nation, C'est Moi: The Encounter of Québec and Aboriginal Nationalisms," *Centre for Constitutional Studies*, 13:3 and 14:1 (2005), 65–79, https://doi.org/10.21991/C9T674.

Chapnick, Adam, "Where Have All of Canada's Diplomatic Historians Gone?" *International Journal* 65, 3 (2010), 725–737. Gale Academic OneFile, link.gale.com/apps/doc/A243452105/AONE?u=learn&sid=bookmark-AONE&xid=c4a7d50e. Accessed May 26, 2025.

Chartrand, Paul, "Self-Determination without a Discrete Territorial Base?" in Donald Clark and Robert Williamson (eds.), *Self-Determination International Perspectives*. London: Macmillan Press, 1996, 302–312.

Christie, Gordon, "Reconciliation in the Face of Crown Intransigence on Indigenous Sovereignty," in Brenda Gunn and Karen Drake (eds.), *Renewing Relationships: Indigenous Peoples and Canada*. Wiyasiwewin Mikiwahp Native Law Centre, University of Saskatchewan, 2019, 20–42.

Clement, William, *The History of the Dominion of Canada*. Toronto: Copp, Clark, 1897.

Considine, Robert, and Joanna Considine, *Healing Our History: The Challenge of the Treaty of Waitangi*, 3rdEd. Auckland: Penguin, 2012.

Coombes, Annie, "Introduction Memory and History in Settler Colonialism," in Annie Coombes (ed.), *Rethinking Settler Colonialism History and Memory in Australia, Canada, Aotearoa New Zealand and South Africa*. Manchester: Manchester University Press, 2006, 1–13.

Coulthard, Glen Sean, *Red Skin, White Masks: Rejecting the Colonial Politics of Recognition*. Minneapolis: University of Minnesota Press, 2014.

Craft, Aimée, *Breathing Life into the Stone Fort Treaty: An Anishnabe Understanding of Treaty One*. Saskatoon: Purich, 2013.

Crawford, Neta, *Argument and Change in World Politics: Ethics, Decolonization, and Humanitarian Intervention*. Cambridge: Cambridge University Press, 2002.

d'Abbs, P., and N. Hewlett, "Explaining Aboriginal Alcohol Use: Changing Perspectives, Hidden Assumptions," in *Learning from 50 Years of Aboriginal Alcohol Programs*. Springer, Singapore. https://doi.org/10.1007/978-981-99-0401-32.

MacDonald, David. "Indigenous Peoples and Self-Determination in Settler States," in Ryan Griffiths, Aleksandar Pavkovic, and Peter Radan (eds.), *The Routledge Handbook on Self-Determination and Secession*. Routledge, 2023, 102–116.

Davis-Delano, Laurel, Renee Galliher, and Joseph Gone, "Absence Makes the Heart Grow Colder: The Harmful Nature of Invisibility of Contemporary American Indians," *Ethnic and Racial Studies*, 47, 15 (2024), 3302–3327, https://doi.org/10.1080/01419870.2024.2308661.

Davis-Delano, Laurel R., Jennifer J. Folsom, Virginia McLaurin, Arianne E. Eason, and Stephanie A. Fryberg, "Representations of Native Americans in U.S. Culture? A Case of Omissions and Commissions," *Social Science Journal* (2021), 1–16. https://doi.org/10.1080/03623319.2021.1975086.

Deer, Sarah, *The Beginning and End of Rape: Confronting Sexual Violence in Native America*. Minneapolis: University of Minnesota Press, 2015.

Defriend, Courtney, and Celeta M. Cook, "Reawakening of Indigenous Matriarchal Systems: A Feminist Approach to Organizational Leadership," *Healthcare Manage Forum* May; 37, 3 (2024), 160–163. https://doi.org/10.1177/08404704231210255.

Deloria Jr, Vine, *Custer Died for Your Sins: An Indian Manifesto*. Norman: University of Oklahoma Press, 1969.

DePasquale, Paul, *Natives and Settlers Now and Then: Historical Issues and Current Perspectives on Treaties and Land Claims in Canada*. Edmonton: University of Alberta Press, 2007.

Dewing, Michael, and Marc Leman, "Canadian Multiculturalism," Ottawa: Library of Parliament Parliamentary Research Branch, 2006. https://publications.gc.ca/collections/Collection-R/LoPBdP/CIR-e/936-1e.pdf.

Dippie, Brian, *The Vanishing American: White Attitudes and U.S. Indian Policy*, Middleton: Wesleyan University Press, 1982.

Duchesne, Ricardo, *Canada in Decay: Mass Immigration, Diversity, and the Ethnocide of Euro-Canadians*. London: Black House, 2018.

Dunbar-Ortiz, Roxanne, and Dina Gilio-Whitaker, *"All the Real Indians Died off": And 20 Other Myths about Native Americans*, Boston: Beacon Press, 2018.

Duncan, David M., *The Prairie Provinces: A Short History of Manitoba, Saskatchewan, and Alberta*. Toronto: W.J. Gage, 1908.

Dunstan, William, "Canadian Indians Today," *Royal Canadian Geographical Society*, 1963.

Ellermann, Antje, *The Comparative Politics of Immigration: Policy Choices in Germany, Canada, Switzerland, and the United States*. Cambridge: Cambridge University Press, 2021.

Environics Institute, "Canadians & Class," September 21, 2023. www.environicsinstitute.org/docs/default-source/default-document-library/cot-2023_reconciliation_relations_with_indigenous_peoples.pdf?sfvrsn=bc7abb12_0.

Environics Institute, "Towards Reconciliation: Indigenous and Non-indigenous Perspectives," October, 2019. www.environicsinstitute.org/docs/default-source/default-document-library/3rd-confed-survey-report-final-oct8.pdf?sfvrsn=246b800_0.

Estes, Nick, *Our History Is the Future: Standing Rock Versus the Dakota Access Pipeline, and the Long Tradition of Indigenous Resistance*. London: Verso Books, 2019.

Evans, Percy, "The History of the Prairie Provinces," in Ashley Brown (ed.), *The Prairie Provinces of Canada: Their History, People, Commerce, Industries, and Resources*. London: Sells, 1914, 13–43.

Federation of Saskatchewan Indian Nations, "Saskatchewan Treaty Land Entitlement," Saskatoon: Federation of Saskatchewan Indians, 2010.

Federation of Saskatchewan Indians, "The Indian Act, The Constitution, Indian Treaties and Indian Government: Position Paper," Saskatoon: Federation of Saskatchewan Indians, July, 1978.

Ferrier, Thompson, *Indian Education in the Northwest*. Toronto: Department of Missionary Literature of the Methodist Church, 1906.

Our Indians and Their Training for Citizenship. Toronto: Department of Missionary Literature of the Methodist Church, 1912.

Fitzgerald, Michael, *Native Americans on Network TV: Stereotypes, Myths, and the "Good Indian."* Lanham: Rowman & Littlefield, 2014.

Flanagan, Tom, *First Nations? Second Thoughts*, 3rd Ed. Montreal: McGill-Queen's University Press, 2019.

Francis, Daniel, *The Imaginary Indian: The Image of the Indian in Canadian Culture*. Vancouver: Arsenal Pulp Press, 1992.

Francis, R. Douglas, and Howard Palmer (eds.), *The Prairie West: Historical Readings*. Pica Pica Press, 1985.

Galloway, Gloria, and Dakshana Bascaramurty, "Census 2016," *Globe and Mail*, 25 October, 2017, https://beta.theglobeandmail.com/news/national/census-2016-highlights-diversity-housing-indigenous/article36711216/?ref=http://www.theglobeandmail.com&.

Gaudry, Adam, and Darryl Leroux, "White Settler Revisionism and Making Métis Everywhere: The Evocation of Métissage in Québec and Nova Scotia," *Critical Ethnic Studies* 3, 1 (2017), 116–142. https://doi.org/10.5749/jcritethnstud.3.1.0116.

George, John, *The Story of Canada Bourinot*, T. Unwin, 1897.

George, Rachel, "Inclusion Is Just the Canadian Word for Assimilation: Self-Determination and the Reconciliation Paradigm in Canada," in Kiera Ladner and Myra Tait (eds.), *Surviving Canada: Indigenous Peoples Celebrate 150 Years of Betrayal*. Winnipeg: Arbeiter Ring, 2017, 49–62.

Gilley, Bruce, *The Case for Colonialism*. London: New English Review Press, 2023.

Glenn, Evelyn, "Settler Colonialism as Structure," *Sociology of Race and Ethnicity* 1,1 (2015), 54–74.

Government of British Columbia, "In Plain Sight: Addressing Indigenous-specific Racism and Discrimination in B.C. Health Care," Vancouver, November, 2020. https://engage.gov.bc.ca/app/uploads/sites/613/2020/11/In-Plain-Sight-Summary-Report.pdf.

Government of Canada, *Annual Report of the Department of Indian Affairs Year Ended 30th June 1907*. Ottawa: Government of Canada, 1907.

Government of Canada, *Annual Report of the Department of Indian Affairs: Year Ended June 30 1904*. Ottawa: Government of Canada, 1905.

Government of Canada, *Annual Report of the Department of Indian Affairs Year Ended 30th June 1897*. Ottawa: Government of Canada, 1898.

Government of Canada, *Annual Report of the Department of Indian Affairs Year Ended 30th June 1889*. Ottawa: Government of Canada, 1890.

Government of Canada, *Canada West*. Ottawa: Department of the Interior, 1914.

Government of Canada, "The Canadian-Indian: A Reference Paper," Ottawa: Department of Citizenship and Immigration Indian Affairs, 1961.

Government of Canada, *Discover Canada: The Rights and Responsibilities of Citizenship*, Ottawa: Department of Immigration, Refugees and Citizenship, 2021, Ci1-11/2021E-PDF.

Government of Canada, "Indians of the Prairie Provinces: An Historical Review," Ottawa: Department of Indian Affairs and Northern Development Canada, March 1967.

Government of Canada, "The Numbered Treaties (1871–1921)," Crown-Indigenous Relations and Northern Affairs Canada, 2023. www.rcaanc-cirnac.gc.ca/eng/1360948213124/1544620003549.

Government of Canada, "Statement by the Ministers of Crown-Indigenous Relations, Indigenous Services, and Northern Affairs on the Catholic Church's rejection of the Doctrine of Discovery," April 1, 2023. www.canada.ca/en/crown-indigenous-relations-northern-affairs/news/2023/03/statement-by-the-ministers-of-indigenous-services-crown-indigenous-relations-and-northern-affairs-on-the-vaticans-rejection-of-the-doctrine-of-disc.html.

Government of Canada, "Treaties and Agreements," *National Public Radio*, 2015. www.npr.org/sections/codeswitch/2015/01/18/368559990/broken-promises-on-display-at-native-american-treaties-exhibit.

Government of Québec, "An Act Respecting the Exercise of the Fundamental Rights and Prerogatives of the Québec People and the Québec State," Québec: Statutes of Québec, E-20.2, 2025. http://legisQuébec.gouv.qc.ca/en/ShowDoc/cs/E-20.2.

Government of Québec, "Ensemble Pour Les Prochaines Générations: Plan D'action Gouvernemental Pour le Mieux-Être Social et Culturel des Premières Nations et des Inuit 2022-2027," Gouvernent de Québec, 2022. https://cdn-contenu.Québec.ca/cdn-contenu/adm/min/conseil-executif/publications-adm/srpni/administratives/plan_action/2022-2027/PAGMSCPNI_22-27.pdf.

Government of Québec, *Our Way of Being Canada: Policy on Québec Affirmation and Canadian Relations*, Québec: Ministère du Conseil Exécutif, 2017.

Gray, Hugh, *Letters from Canada, Written during a Residence There in the Years 1806, 1807, and 1808*. London: Longman, Hurst, Rees, and Orne, 1809.

Gray, Andrew, "Onion Lake and the Revitalisation of Treaty Six," in *Honour Bound: Onion Lake and the Spirit of Treaty Six*. Copenhagen: International Work Group for Indigenous Affairs, 1997, 19–56.

Hayward, Mark, *Identity and Industry: Making Media Multicultural in Canada*, Montreal: McGill-Queen's University Press, 2019.

Heaman, Elsbeth, *Civilization: From Enlightenment Philosophy to Canadian History*. Montreal: McGill-Queen's University Press, 2022.

Henderson, James Sakej Youngblood, "Empowering Treaty Federalism" *Saskatchewan Law Review* 58, 2 (1994): 241–330.

Hoehn, Felix, *Reconciling Sovereignties: Aboriginal Nations and Canada*. Saskatoon: University of Saskatchewan Native Law Center, 2012.

Holy See, "Joint Statement of the Dicasteries for Culture and Education and for Promoting Integral Human Development on the 'Doctrine of Discovery'," March 30, 2023, Holy See Press Office, https://press.vatican.va/content/salastampa/en/bollettino/pubblico/2023/03/30/230330b.html.

Hopkins, John, *The Story of the Dominion: Four Hundred Years in the Annals of Half a Continent*. Toronto: John C. Winston, 1901.

Indian Association of Alberta, *Citizens Plus: The Red Paper*. Edmonton: Indian Association of Alberta, 1970.

Innes, Robert Alexander, "Historians and Indigenous Genocide in Saskatchewan," June 21, 2018, https://shekonneechie.ca/2018/06/21/historians-and-indigenous-genocide-in-saskatchewan/.

Jackson, Moana, "Decolonisation and the Stories in the Land," *E-Tangata*, 21 May, 2021. https://e-tangata.co.nz/comment-and-analysis/moana-jackson-decolonisation-and-the-stories-in-the-land/.

Jai, Julie, "Bargains Made in Bad Times: How Principles from Modern Treaties Can Reinvigorate Historic Treaties," in John Borrows and Michael Coyle (eds.), *The Right Relationship: Reimagining the Implementation of Historical Treaties*. Toronto: University of Toronto Press, 2017, 105–139.

Jenness, Diamond, *The Indians of Canada 6th Ed*. Ottawa: National Museum of Canada Bulletin 65 Anthropological Series No. 15, 1963.

Johnson, Harold, *Two Families: Treaties and Government*, Saskatoon: Purich, 2007.

Joseph, Bob, *Dispelling Myths about Indigenous Peoples*. Vancouver: Indigenous Corporate Training, 2019.

Kennedy, Howard Angus, *The Book of the West*. Toronto: Ryerson Press, 1925.

Khong, Yuen Foong, *Analogies at War: Korea, Munich, Dien Bien Phu, and the Vietnam Decisions of 1965*. Princeton: Princeton University Press, 1992.

Kidd, Kenneth E., *Canadians of Long Ago: The Story of The Canadian Indian*. Toronto: Longmans, Green, 1951.

Krasowski, Sheldon, *No Surrender: The Land Remains Indigenous*. Regina: University of Regina Press, 2019.

Kuokkanen, Rauna, *Restructuring Relations: Indigenous Self-Determination, Governance, and Gender*. Oxford: Oxford University Press, 2019.

Kymlicka, Will, "Being Canadian," in Karen Wendling (ed.), *Ethics in Canada: Ethical, Social and Political Perspectives*. Oxford: Oxford University Press, 2015, 171–187.

Ladner, Kiera L., "Take 35: Reconciling Constitutional Orders," in Annie-Marie Timpson (ed.), *First Nations, First Thoughts: The Impact of Indigenous Thought in Canada*. Vancouver: University of British Columbia Press, 2009, 279–300.

"Treaty Federalism: An Indigenous Vision of Canadian Federalism," in François Rocher and Miriam Smith (eds.), *New Trends in Canadian Federalism*. Peterborough: Broadview Press, 2003, 167–196.

Laidlaw, Ronald, "European Settlement and Aboriginal Society," in Ted Gurry (ed.), *The European Occupation*. Richmond: Heinemann Educational, 1984.

Lalonde, Michelle, "Systematic Erasure: Indigenous Leaders Reject Legault's Comments on Québec," *Montreal Gazette*, June 1, 2024. https://montrealgazette.com/news/Québec/first-nations-leaders-francois-legault-Québec-national-history-museum.

Lawrence, Bonita, "Gender, Race, and the Regulation of Native Identity in Canada and the United States," *Hypatia* 18, 2 (2003), 3–31.

Lawrence, Bonita, and Enakshi Dua, "Decolonizing Anti-racism," *Social Justice* 32, 4 (2005), 120–143.

Laxer, Emily, *Unveiling the Nation: The Politics of Secularism in France and Québec*, Montreal: McGill-Queen's University Press, 2019.

Leacock, Stephen, *Canada: The Foundations of Its Future*. Montreal: House of Seagram, 1941.

Leroux, Darryl, *Distorted Descent: White Claims to Indigenous Identity*. Winnipeg: University of Manitoba Press, 2020.

"The Many Paradoxes of Race in Québec: Civilization, Laïité and Gender Equality," in Lynn Caldwell, Darryl Leroux, and Carrianne Leung (eds.), *Critical Inquiries: A Reader in Studies of Canada*. Halifax: Fernwood, 2013, 53–70.

Lightfoot, Sheryl, *Global Indigenous Politics: A Subtle Revolution*. New York: Routledge, 2016.

Lipsitz, George, *The Possessive Investment in Whiteness: How White People Profit from Identity Politics*. Philadelphia: Temple University Press, 2018.

Livingstone, Anne-Marie, "Racism versus Culture: Competing Interpretations of Racial Inequality in Canadian Public Policy," *Ethnic and Racial Studies*, 47, 6 (2023), 1329–1350. https://doi.org/10.1080/01419870.2023.2248237.

Lopez, Julisa, Arianne Eason, and Stephanie Fryberg, "The Same, Yet Different: Understanding the Perceived Acceptability of Redface and Blackface," *Social Psychological and Personality Science* 13, 3 (2022), 698–709. https://doi.org/10.1177/19485506211039906.

Lowrie, Morgan, "After Indigenous Criticism, Legault Defends New Museum on Québécois Nation," *Global News*, 2024. https://globalnews.ca/news/10482799/Québec-legault-museum-indigenous-criticism/.

Lowrie, Morgan, "Historians, First Nations Leader Question Québec History Museum Concept," *Global News*, 2024. https://globalnews.ca/news/10491401/historians-first-nations-question-Québec-history-museum/.

Lucas, Charles, *A Historical Geography of the British Colonies: Vol. V Canada*. Oxford: Clarendon Press, 1901.

MacDonald, David, "Canada's History War: Indigenous Genocide and Public Memory in the United States, Australia, and Canada," *Journal of Genocide Research* 17, 4 (2015), 411–431. https://doi.org/10.1080/14623528.2015.1096583.

MacDonald, David, "Canada's Truth and Reconciliation Commission: Assessing Context, Process, and Critiques," *Griffith Law Review* 29, 1 (2020), 150–174. https://doi.org/10.1080/10383441.2020.1868282.

MacDonald, David, *Identity Politics in the Age of Genocide*. London: Routledge, 2008.

MacDonald, David, "Match and Exceed: Why Recognizing Genocide in Canada Is Only the First Step in Promoting Indigenous Self-Determination," in David MacDonald and Emily Grafton (eds.), *Critical Engagements with Settler Colonialism in Canada*. Regina: University of Regina Press, 2025.

MacDonald, David, "Paved with Comfortable Intentions: Moving beyond Liberal Multiculturalism and Civil Rights Frames on the Road to Transformative Reconciliation," in Aimée Craft and Paulette Regan (eds.), *Pathways to Reconciliation*. Winnipeg: University of Manitoba Press, 2020, 577–597.

MacDonald, D. B. *The Sleeping Giant Awakens: Genocide, Indian Residential Schools, and the Challenge of Conciliation*, University of Toronto Press, 256.

MacDonald, Liana, *Silencing and Institutional Racism in Settler-Colonial Education*. PhD thesis, Victoria University of Wellington, 2018.

MacIntyre, Stuart, and Anna Clark, *The History Wars*. Melbourne: Melbourne University Press, 2004.

Mackey, Eva. *The House of Difference: Cultural Politics and National Identity in Canada*. Toronto: University of Toronto Press, 2002.

MacKinnon, Catou, "AFN's Québec and Labrador Chief Tells Viens Inquiry 'Systemic Discrimination' Must be Addressed," *CBC News*, 2017, www.cbc.ca/news/canada/montreal/viens-inquiry-ghislain-picard-1.4147951.

Maclean, John, *Canadian Savage Folk: The Native Tribes of Canada*. Toronto: William Briggs, 1896.

Maclean John, *The Indians of Canada*. London: Charles H. Kelly, 1892.

Manuel, Arthur, and Ronald Derrickson, *The Reconciliation Manifesto: Recovering the Land and Rebuilding the Economy*. Toronto: Lorimer, 2017.

Mcgullagh, John, *Red Indians I Have Known*. London: Church Missionary Society, 1919.

McLane, Patrick, Leslee Mackey, Brian R. Holroyd, et al., "Impacts of Racism on First Nations Patients' Emergency Care," *BMC Health Services Research* 22, 804 (2022), 5–6. https://doi.org/10.1186/s12913-022-08129-5.

Mclean, Sheelah, "'We Built a Life from Nothing': White Settler Colonialism and the Myth of Meritocracy," *Os*, 2018. https://canadacommons.ca/artifacts/2139424/we-built-a-life-from-nothing/2894721/.

McMullin, John, *History of Canada*. Brockville: John McMullin, 1855.

Mellick, Henry George, *The Indians and Our Indian Missions*. Winnipeg: HC Stovel, 1909.

Mercer, Adam, and Robertson, William John, *History Primer: Public School History of England and Canada*. Toronto: Copp, Clark, 1886.

Miller, Robert J., Jacinta Ruru, Larissa Behrendt, and Tracey Lindberg, *Discovering Indigenous Lands*. Oxford: Oxford University Press, 2010.

Minogue, Kenneth, "Aborigines and Australian Apologetics," *Quadrant*, September, 1998, 13–15.

Monchalin, Lisa, *The Colonial Problem: An Indigenous Perspective on Crime and Injustice in Canada*. Toronto: University of Toronto Press, 2016.

Moreau, Claudia, Jean-François Lefebvre, Michèle Jomphe et al. "Native American admixture in the Québec founder population," *PLoS One* 8, 6 (2013), 1–9, e65507. https://doi.org/10.1371/journal.pone.0065507.

Morgan, Cecilia, *Commemorating Canada: History, Heritage, and Memory, 1850s–1990s*. Toronto: University of Toronto Press, 2016.

Morrison, T. G., M. A. Morrison, and T. Borsa, "A Legacy of Derogation: Prejudice toward Aboriginal Persons in Canada," *Psychology* 5, (2014), 1001–1010. https://doi.org/10.4236/psych.2014.59112.

Morrison, Melanie A., Todd G. Morrison, Rebecca L. Harriman, and Linda M. Jewell, (2008). "Old-fashioned and Modern Prejudice toward Aboriginals in Canada," in Melanie A. Morrison and Todd G. Morrison (eds.), *The Psychology of Modern Prejudice*. New York: Nova Science, 2008, 277–305.

Moreton-Robinson, Aileen, *The White Possessive: Property, Power, and Indigenous Sovereignty*. Minneapolis: University of Minnesota Press, 2015.

Moses, A. Dirk, *Genocide and Settler Society: Frontier Violence and Stolen Indigenous Children in Australian History*. New York: Berghahn Books, 2004.

Moss, Wendy, and Elaine Gardner-O'Toole, *Aboriginal People: History of Discriminatory Laws*, Law and Government Division, Ottawa Library of Parliament, November, 1991, http://publications.gc.ca/Collection-R/LoPBdP/BP/bp175-e.html.

National Indian Brotherhood, *Aboriginal People of Canada and Their Environment, Rev. Ed*. Ottawa ON: National Indian Brotherhood, 1973.

National Inquiry into Missing and Murdered Indigenous Women and Girls, *Reclaiming Power and Place: The Final Report of the National Inquiry into Missing and Murdered Indigenous Women and Girls: Volume 1a*. Vancouver: Privy Council Office, 2019.

Newcomb, Steven, "Domination in Relation to Indigenous ('Dominated') Peoples in International law," in Irene Watson (ed.), *Indigenous Peoples as Subjects of International Law*. London: Routledge Press, 2017, 18–37.

Nichols, Robert, "Indigeneity and the Settler Contract Today," *Philosophy and Social Criticism* 39, 2 (2013), 165–186. https://doi.org/10.1177/0191453712470359.

O'Sullivan, Dominic, "Treaties, Truth and Equality: How NZ, Australia and Canada Are All Struggling with Colonial Politics," *The Conversation*, November 18, 2024, https://theconversation.com/treaties-truth-and-equality-how-nz-australia-and-canada-are-all-struggling-with-colonial-politics-243575.

Office of the Special Interlocutor, *Sites of Truth, Sites of Conscience Unmarked Burials and Mass Graves of Missing and Disappeared Indigenous Children in Canada*. Ottawa: Office of the Independent Special Interlocutor for Missing Children and Unmarked Graves and Burial Sites associated with Indian Residential Schools, 2024.

Ostler, Jeffrey, *Surviving Genocide: Native Nations and the United States from the American Revolution to Bleeding Kansas*. New Haven: Yale University Press, 2019.

Palmater, Pamela D., *Beyond Blood: Rethinking Indigenous Identity*. Vancouver: University of British Columbia Press, 2011.

Palmater, Pamela, *Indigenous Nationhood: Empowering Grassroots Citizens*. Halifax: Fernwood, 2015.

Plover, Adam, *New Zealand: The Benefits of Colonisation*. Wellington: Tross, 2022.

Pool, Ian, *Te Iwi Māori: A New Zealand Population*. Auckland: Auckland University Press, 1991.

Québec, Bill 84, An Act respecting integration into the Québec nation (modified title) 28 May 2025 Assemblée nationale du Québec »https://www.assnat.qc.ca/en/travaux-parlementaires/projets-loi/projet-loi-84-43-1.html.

Ralph, Julian, *On Canada's Frontier: Sketches of History, Sport, and Adventure and of the Indians, Missionaries Fur-Traders, and Newer Settlers of Western Canada*. New York: Harper & Brothers, 1892.

Razack, Sherene, *Dying from Improvement: Inquests and Inquiries into Indigenous Deaths in Custody*. Toronto: University of Toronto Press, 2015.

Reading, Charlotte, "Understanding Racism," Collaborating Centre for Indigenous Health (NCCIH), 2013. www.nccah-ccnsa.ca/Publications/Lists/Publications/Attachments/103/understanding_racism_EN_web.pdf.

Redsky, A., B. Young, L. Brown, and M. Buss, "Report on Core Elements of Anti-Indigenous Racism Policies and Processes," Ottawa: National Consortium for Indigenous Medical Education, 2024. https://ncime.ca/wp-content/uploads/2024/06/Report-on-Core-Elements-of-Anti-Indigenous-Racism-Policies-and-Processes-2.pdf.

Regan, Paulette, *Unsettling the Settler within: Indian Residential Schools, Truth Telling, and Reconciliation in Canada*. Vancouver: University of British Columbia Press, 2010.

Rifkin, Mark, *Settler Common Sense: Queerness and Everyday Colonialism in the American Renaissance*. Minneapolis: University of Minnesota Press, 2014.

Rollings-Magnusson, Sandra, *The Homesteaders*. Regina: University of Regina Press, 2018.

Rudin, Ronald, *Making History in Twentieth-Century Québec*. Toronto: University of Toronto Press, 1997.

Russell, Peter, *Constitutional Odyssey: Can Canadians be a Sovereign People*. Toronto: University of Toronto Press, 2004.

Salée, Daniel, "The New Face of Québec Nationalism: Reconsidering the Nationalism/Democracy Nexus," *American Review of Canadian Studies* 52, 2, 2022, 119–138. https://doi.org/10.1080/02722011.2022.2067733.

Savoie, Donald J., *Canada: Beyond Grudges, Grievances, and Disunity*. Montreal: McGill-Queen's University Press, 2023.

Schaefli, Laura., Anne Godlewska, and Christopher Lamb, "Securing Indigenous Dispossession through Education: An Analysis of Canadian Curricula and Textbooks," in Holger Jahnke, Caroline Kramer, Peter Meusburger, (eds.), *Geographies of Schooling: Knowledge and Space*, Springer, 2019, 145–154.

Scott, Joseph, *The Story of Our Prairie Provinces*. Toronto: J.M. Dent and Sons, 1943.

Sharma, Nandita, "Canadian Multiculturalism and Its Nationalism," in May Chazan, Lisa Helps, Anna Stanley, Sonali Thakkar. (eds.), *Home and Native Land: Unsettling Multiculturalism in Canada.* Toronto: Between the Lines, 2011, 85–101.

Simpson, Audra, *Mohawk Interruptus: Political Life across the Borders of Settler States.* Durham: Duke University Press, 2014.

Simpson, Leanne Betasamosake, *As We Have Always Done: Indigenous Freedom through Radical Resistance.* Minneapolis: University of Minnesota Press, 2017.

Simpson, Leanne Betasamosake, and Robyin Maynard, *Rehearsals for Living,* Chicago: Haymarket, 2022.

Simpson, Leanne Betasamosake, Rinaldo Walcott, and Glen Coulthard, "Idle No More and Black Lives Matter: An Exchange," *Studies in Social Justice* 12, 1 (2018), 75–89.

Sinclair, Keith, *A Destiny Apart: New Zealand's Search for National Identity.* Auckland: Allen & Unwin, 1986.

Singh, Anneliese A., *The Racial Healing Handbook.* Oakland, CA: New Harbinger, 2019.

Slattery, Brian, *Ancestral Lands, Alien Laws: Judicial Perspectives on Aboriginal Title.* Saskatoon: University of Saskatchewan Native Law Centre, 1983.

Smits, David D., "The 'Squaw Drudge': A Prime Index of Savagism," *Ethnohistory,* 29, 4 (1982), 281–306.

Spence, Thomas, *The Prairie Lands of Canada.* Montreal: Gazette Printing, 1879.

Starblanket, Gina, "Red Ticket Women: Revisiting the Political Contributions of the Indian Rights for Indian Women's Movement," in Gina Starblanket (ed.), *Making Space for Indigenous Feminism, 3rd Ed.* Halifax: Fernwood, 2024.

Starblanket, Gina, "The Numbered Treaties and the Politics of Incoherency," *Canadian Journal of Political Science* 52, 3 (2019), 443–459.

Starblanket, Gina, and Dallas Hunt, *Storying Violence: Unravelling Colonial Narratives in the Stanley Trial.* Winnipeg: Arbeiter Ring, 2020.

Stark, Heidi Kiiwetinepinesiik, "Criminal Empire: The Making of the Savage in a Lawless Land," *Theory & Event* 19,4 (2016).

Statistics Canada, "Indigenous population continues to grow and is much younger than the non-Indigenous population, although the pace of growth has slowed," 2022. www150.statcan.gc.ca/n1/daily-quotidien/220921/dq220921a-eng.htm?indid=32990-1&indgeo=0.

Steeves, Paulette, *The Indigenous Paleolithic of the Western Hemisphere.* Lincoln: University of Nebraska Press, 2021.

Taylor, M. Brook, *Promoters, Patriots, and Partisans: Historiography in Nineteenth-Century English Canada*. Toronto: University of Toronto Press, 1989.

Te Punga Somerville, Alice, *Two Hundred and Fifty Ways to Start an Essay about Captain Cook*. Auckland: Bridget Williams Books, 2020.

Thobani, Sunera, *Exalted Subjects*. Toronto: University of Toronto Press, 2007.

Tobias, John, "Protection, Civilization, Assimilation: An Outline History of Canada's Indian Policy," *The Western Canadian Journal of Anthropology* 6, 2 (1976), 13–19.

Trudeau, Pierre, "Canadian Culture," *Hansard* October 8, 1971. www.lipad.ca/full/1971/10/08/1/.

Truth and Reconciliation Commission of Canada, *Final Report of the Truth and Reconciliation Commission of Canada, Volume One: Summary: Honouring the Truth, Reconciling for the Future*. Winnipeg: Truth and Reconciliation Commission, 2015.

Tuck, Eve, "Suspending Damage: A Letter to Communities," *Harvard Educational Review* 7, 3 (2009), 409–428. https://doi.org/10.17763/haer.79.3.n0016675661t3n15.

Tucker, Norman, *The Protection of Native Races*. Vancouver: The Canadian Association of Friends of Native Races, 1914.

Tudor, Henry, *Political Myth*. London: Macmillan, 1972.

Turner, Dale, *This Is Not a Peace Pipe: Towards a Critical Indigenous Philosophy*. Toronto: University of Toronto Press, 2005.

Venne, Sharon, "Introduction," in *Honour Bound: Onion Lake and the Spirit of Treaty Six*. Copenhagen: International Work Group for Indigenous Affairs, 1997, 5–9.

Venne, Sharon, "Treaties Made in Good Faith," in Paul DePasquale (ed.), *Natives and Settlers Now and Then: Historical Issues and Current Perspectives on Treaties and Land Claims in Canada*. Edmonton: University of Alberta Press, 2007, 1–17.

Veracini, Lorenzo, "The Cost of Reconciliation: Distinguishing Colonialism and Settler Colonialism," *Intotemak Magazine* Special Issue 2016, 79–81.

Vimalassery, Manu, Juliana Hu Pegues, and Alyosha Goldstein, "Colonial Unknowing and Relations of Study," *Theory & Event* 20, 4 (2017), 1042–1054.

Vowel, Chelsea, *Indigenous Writes: A Guide to First Nations, Métis, and Inuit Issues in Canada*. Winnipeg: HighWater Press, 2016.

Walters, Mark, "Constitutive Power and the Nation(s) of Québec," in Richard Albert and Léonid Sirota (eds.), *A Written Constitution for Québec*. Montreal: McGill-Queen's University Press, 2023, 162–188.

Wang, Hansi Lo, "Broken Promises on Display at Native American Treaties Exhibit," *Code Switch / National Public Radio*. January 18, 2015. www.npr.org/sections/codeswitch/2015/01/18/368559990/broken-promises-on-display-at-native-american-treaties-exhibit.

Warburton, George, *The Conquest of Canada*. London: Richard Bentley, 1857.

Weaver, Emily, *A Canadian History for Boys and Girls*. Toronto: Copp Clark, 1919.

Widdowson, Frances, and Albert Howard, *Disrobing the Aboriginal Industry: The Deception behind Indigenous Cultural Preservation*. Montreal: Queens-McGill University Press, 2008.

Williams, Ernest Edwin, *The Imperial Heritage*. London: Ward, Lock, 1898.

Wilson, James, *The Earth Shall Weep: A History of Native America*, New York: Atlantic Monthly Press, 1998.

Wolfe, Patrick, "Settler Colonialism and the Elimination of the Native," *Journal of Genocide Research* 8, 4 (2006), 387–409.

Woolf, Daniel, *A Concise History of History: Global Historiography from Antiquity to the Present*. Cambridge: Cambridge University Press, 2019.

Wrong, George, *Canada and the American Revolution*. Toronto: MacMillan Canada, 1935.

Wylie, Lloy, and Stephanie McConkey, "Insiders' Insight: Discrimination against Indigenous Peoples through the Eyes of Health Care Professionals," *Journal of Racial and Ethnic Health Disparities* 6 (2019), 37–45. https://doi.org/10.1007/s40615-018-0495-9.

Yellowhead Institute, "Treaty-Making Is Older than Canada," Toronto: York University, 2024. https://treatymap.yellowheadinstitute.org/map/.

Zakaras, Alex, *The Roots of American Individualism: Political Myth in the Age of Jackson*, Princeton: Princeton University Press, 2022.

Zerubavel, Eviatar, *The Elephant in the Room: Silence and Denial in Everyday Life*. Oxford: Oxford University Press, 2005.

Acknowledgements

Thank you to Daniel Woolf, Amitava Chowdhury, Michael Cachagee, Sheryl Lightfoot, Andrew Woolford, Desmond McAllister, Tony Barta, Murray Sinclair, Paulette Regan, Tricia Logan, Priscilla Settee, Shelagh Rogers, Karine Duhamel, and Emily Grafton. Three anonymous reviewers have made this a much better Element. Thank you to my parents, Olive and Bruce, and sister, Rachel. My special thanks to my wife Dana and son Gulliver. This research was funded by Social Sciences and Humanities Research Council of Canada Insight Grant 430855.

Cambridge Elements

Historical Theory and Practice

Daniel Woolf
Queen's University, Ontario

Daniel Woolf is Professor of History at Queen's University, where he served for ten years as Principal and Vice-Chancellor, and has held academic appointments at a number of Canadian universities. He is the author or editor of several books and articles on the history of historical thought and writing, and on early modern British intellectual history, including most recently *A Concise History of History* (CUP 2019). He is a Fellow of the Royal Historical Society, the Royal Society of Canada, and the Society of Antiquaries of London. He is married with three adult children.

Editorial Board

Dipesh Chakrabarty, *University of Chicago*
Marnie Hughes-Warrington, *University of South Australia*
Ludmilla Jordanova, *University of Durham*
Angela McCarthy, *University of Otago*
María Inés Mudrovcic, *Universidad Nacional de Comahue*
Herman Paul, *Leiden University*
Stefan Tanaka, *University of California, San Diego*
Richard Ashby Wilson, *University of Connecticut*

About the Series

Cambridge Elements in Historical Theory and Practice is a series intended for a wide range of students, scholars, and others whose interests involve engagement with the past. Topics include the theoretical, ethical, and philosophical issues involved in doing history, the interconnections between history and other disciplines and questions of method, and the application of historical knowledge to contemporary global and social issues such as climate change, reconciliation and justice, heritage, and identity politics.

Cambridge Elements

Historical Theory and Practice

Elements in the Series

Writing the History of Global Slavery
Trevor Burnard

Plural Pasts: Historiography between Events and Structures
Arthur Alfaix Assis

The History of Knowledge
Johan Östling and David Larsson Heidenblad

Conceptualizing the History of the Present Time
María Inés Mudrovcic

Writing the History of the African Diaspora
Toyin Falola

Dealing with Dark Pasts: A European History of Auto-Critical Memory in Global Perspective
Itay Lotem

A Human Rights View of the Past
Antoon De Baets

Historians' Autobiographies as Historiographical Inquiry: A Global Perspective
Jaume Aurell

Historiographic Reasoning
Aviezer Tucker

Pragmatism and Historical Representation
Serge Grigoriev

History and Hermeneutics
Paul Fairfield

Myths, History Wars, and Indigenous–Settler Relations in Canada and Other Settler States
David Bruce Amichand MacDonald

A full series listing is available at: www.cambridge.org/EHTP

For EU product safety concerns, contact us at Calle de José Abascal, 56–1°, 28003 Madrid, Spain or eugpsr@cambridge.org.